Microsoft® Windows® XP
Media Center Edition
fast&easy™

Eric D. Grebler

Premier
Press

The Premier Press logo and related trade dress are trademarks of Premier Press and may not be used without written permission.

Publisher: Stacy L. Hiquet
Senior Marketing Manager: Sarah O'Donnell
Marketing Manager: Heather Hurley
Associate Marketing Manager: Kristin Eisenzopf
Retail Market Coordinator: Sarah Dubois
Manager of Editorial Services: Heather Talbot
Project Editor/Proofreader: Megan Belanger
Technical Reviewer: Greg Perry
Copy Editor: Sandi Wilson
Interior Layout: Danielle Foster
Cover Designer: Mike Tanamachi
Indexer: Kelly Talbot

Microsoft, Windows, Internet Explorer, and Outlook are either registered trademarks or trademarks of Microsoft Corporation in the United States and/or other countries.

All other trademarks are the property of their respective owners.

Important: Premier Press cannot provide software support. Please contact the appropriate software manufacturer's technical support line or Web site for assistance.

Premier Press and the author have attempted throughout this book to distinguish proprietary trademarks from descriptive terms by following the capitalization style used by the manufacturer.

Information contained in this book has been obtained by Premier Press from sources believed to be reliable. However, because of the possibility of human or mechanical error by our sources, Premier Press, or others, the Publisher does not guarantee the accuracy, adequacy, or completeness of any information and is not responsible for any errors or omissions or the results obtained from use of such information. Readers should be particularly aware of the fact that the Internet is an ever-changing entity. Some facts may have changed since this book went to press.

ISBN: 1-59200-083-5
Library of Congress Catalog Card Number: 2003105356
Printed in the United States of America
03 04 05 06 07 BH 10 9 8 7 6 5 4 3 2 1

Premier Press, a division of Course Technology
25 Thomson Place
Boston, MA 02210

Acknowledgments

The process of writing a book typically involves the efforts of many people. Not so in this case—I did it all by myself! But seriously, folks… (my dreams of being a stand-up comic faded long ago, so please indulge me).

Special thanks must be extended to my wife Kara, whose love, devotion, and support is always an inspiration to me. Who I am today is a direct reflection of the care and nurturing of my parents Rivka and Victor, who have always supported me in all my endeavors. Thanks to my brothers; to Ron, who was the best computer-programming partner (our Bats game could've given Nintendo a run for their money), and to Oren and Leor, who may have knocked some sense into me when they ganged up and knocked me out. (No need to call family services, it was an "accident.")

Thanks to the people at HP who generously provided the test system for this book.

Thanks to all my friends and family who add a wonderful element to my life. Typically, a person's list of friends would be too long to thank in a format like this; luckily that's not the case for me. Special thanks to Rob Blier and Chris Gray, who are a much-needed outlet for venting, eating, and golfing. Also, thanks to my fan club members, including Anthony, Erynn, Ron, Meredith, Evan, Grant, Marge, Yehiel, Safta, Daryl, Alysa, Jay, Cliff, Danielle, Kevin, Jenbird, Sam, and Diana.

Thanks to Stacy Hiquet and all of the Premier Press team, including my editors Megan Belanger and Sandi Wilson, for helping me bring this book to life.

About the Author

Eric D. Grebler is an IT professional, author, and certified trainer who has demystified the world of computers for thousands of people. He has developed curriculum and resource material on a wide range of technical topics. Eric is also the author of *CorelDRAW for Linux* from Premier Press (formerly Prima Publishing) and *Lindows Fast & Easy* from Premier Press.

When he's not busy leading vocals for living-room karaoke, Eric spends much of his time counting calories and figuring out ways to melt away the fat. Every day he gets closer to reaching his goal of either being on the cover of a muscle magazine or becoming a lounge singer.

Contents

Introduction

This *Fast & Easy* book from Premier Press is a great tool for those exploring the world of the Windows XP Media Center Edition PC, one of the latest technology innovations in computing. Windows XP Media Center Edition is an operating system that truly keeps up with the demands of today's multimedia-hungry computer users. It was designed for users who want to get the most out of the investment they made in their computer.

For years, people have been combining technologies to make life easier. I have a watch that is also a remote control, a camera that doubles as an MP3 player, and a pen that is also a clock. It's no wonder that there are now computers that act as televisions, VCRs, DVDs, and CD players. Windows XP Media Center Edition brings together all of these technologies in an easy-to-use operating system that can control all of your multimedia devices at the touch of a button.

Windows XP Media Center Edition comes preinstalled on Media Center computers that are currently available from a variety of different manufacturers. It is primarily the operating system Windows XP with some additional functionality. This additional functionality comes mainly in the form of the Media Center. The Media Center is a program that allows you to control the built-in television, program guide, recorder, video player, DVD player, CD player, and photo viewer. It also acts as a central location to manage all of your multimedia files. An added bonus of Windows XP Media Center computers is that they come with a remote control that will allow you to control your computer from a distance. This makes the transition from watching television in the traditional way to watching it on your computer even easier.

Obviously, no book can really teach you everything there is to know about any one topic. The goal of this book is to provide you with a "fast and easy" way to perform the most common tasks with your Windows XP Media Center Edition computer. Each task is divided into step-by-step instructions accompanied by screen shots that will make following those steps even easier.

Who Should Read This Book?

Whether you are a first-time computer user or a seasoned veteran, there is a benefit in this book for you. Because the Media Center is a new technology, even people with a lot of computer experience can benefit from this book. It can be used either as a learning tool or as a reference guide. If you are stuck on a particular task, you can quickly look it up in the book and follow the step-by-step instructions for accomplishing that task. If you are new to computing, you can select any chapter and follow the steps to get a better understanding of how to accomplish things on your computer. As the chapters don't necessarily build on one another, you can start at any point of interest.

Some Helpful Hints

In addition to the step-by-step instructions, you'll notice that there are two other elements designed to help you:

TIP

Tips provide you with quick ways or shortcuts to perform certain tasks.

NOTE

Notes provide you with additional information or background on a particular topic.

1

Getting Started with the Media Center

My dad built the first computer that we ever owned. It was basically a motherboard with a membrane keypad, 8k of memory, and an LED readout. If you don't know much about computers, comparing that machine to the Windows XP Media Center Edition computer is like comparing a go-cart to an F16 fighter plane. Your Windows XP Media Center computer is like no other you've used before. Not only is it a fully functioning, powerful computer, it also doubles as your TV, VCR, DVD, and CD player. It's so advanced that it lets you pause and rewind live programming, tape shows, sort music and videos, and do so much more. The Media Center is the heart of the entertainment on your computer. It is a separate area from the rest of your computer that will allow you to control all of the multimedia functionality of your machine. The first step once you've turned on your computer is to set up and get to know the Media Center. In this chapter, you'll learn how to:

- Set up the Media Center
- Navigate the Media Center

First Run Wizard

The first time you start the Media Center, you will be taken through the First Run Wizard that will allow you to configure the Media Center. Step by step, you will be asked to provide information so that your computer can be properly configured. You will need to have your remote control handy in order to go through the First Run Wizard.

1. Click Start. The Start menu will appear.

2. Click Media Center. The Media Center will launch in a separate window and the First Run Wizard will begin.

3. Click Next. The process of setting up the Media Center will begin.

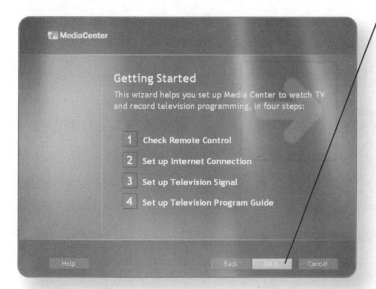

4. Click Next. This will advance you to the remote control setup screen.

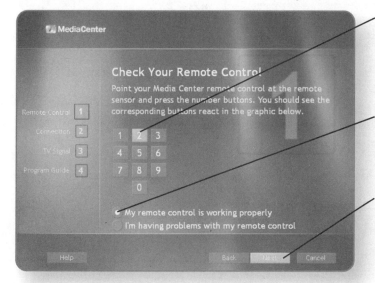

5. Press any number on the remote control. As you press a numbered button, the corresponding number should react on the screen.

6. Click in the **circle** beside **My remote control is working properly.** A dot will appear in the circle, once selected.

7. Click Next to advance to the next page of the First Run Wizard. Alternatively, you can use the remote control to navigate through the rest of the wizard.

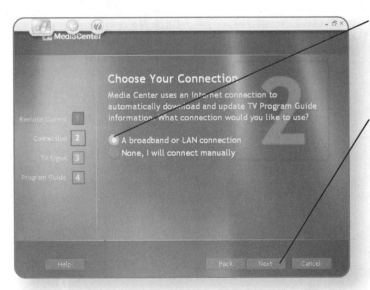

8. **Click** in the **circle** beside the **desired option** for connecting to the Internet. A dot will appear beside the selection that you have chosen.

9. **Click Next** to proceed to the next page.

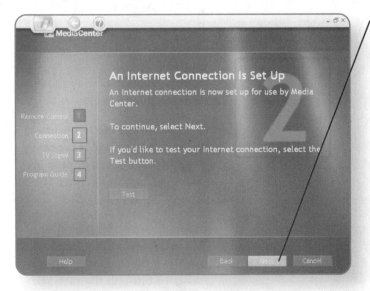

10. **Click Next** to proceed to the next screen in the wizard.

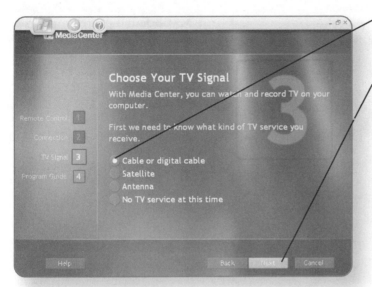

11. **Click** in the **circle** beside the **type of Internet connection** that you have.

12. **Click Next** to advance to the next screen of the wizard.

NOTE

To set up the Program Guide function, you must first be connected to the Internet.

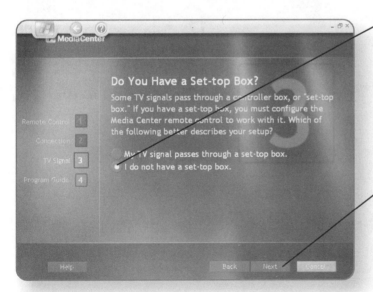

13. **Click** in the **circle** beside **I do not have a set-top box**, unless your TV signal does pass through a set-top box. If you do have a set-top box, there will be an additional screen where you will have to input some information about your set-top box.

14. **Click Next** to proceed to the Terms of Service page.

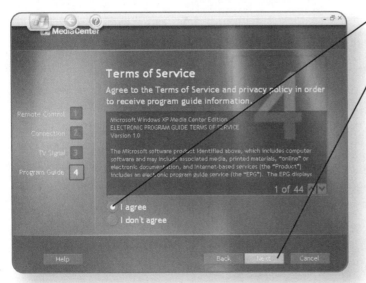

15. **Click** in the **circle** beside **I agree**. A dot will appear in the circle.

16. **Click Next** to proceed to the Guide setup.

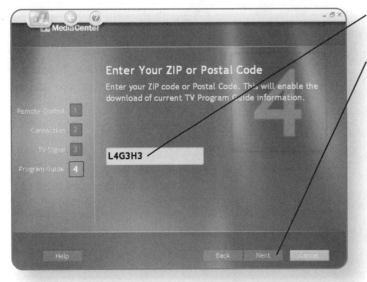

17. **Type** in **your Postal or ZIP Code**. It will appear as you type.

18. **Click Next**. The Program Guide will now be set up.

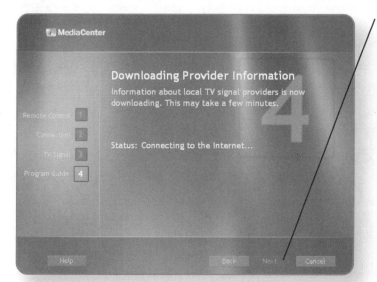

19. **Click Next** after the download is complete.

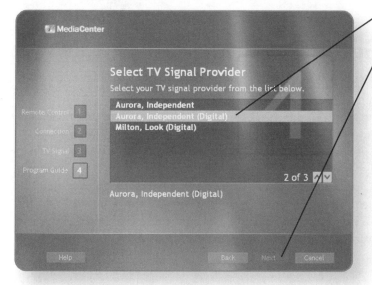

20. **Click** on the **desired TV signal provider**.

21. **Click Next**. The Program Guide information will be downloaded.

NOTE

In order for the Television Guide function to work properly, you must select the correct signal provider. If you are unsure of the correct selection, call your local cable provider to find out.

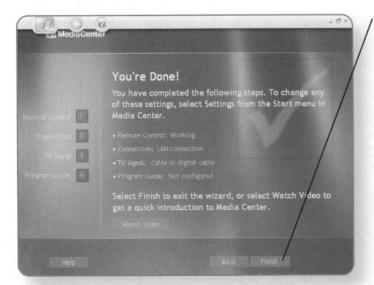

22. **Click Finish**. The setup of Media Center is now complete.

Getting to Know the Media Center

The Media Center has built-in navigational controls that will allow you to get around easily. These navigational controls will appear when you hover your mouse anywhere over the Media Center window. If your mouse does not move for 5 seconds, the navigational controls will disappear until you move your mouse again. This is particularly useful when you are watching TV, as you don't want the navigational controls to block part of the screen and interfere with your television-watching experience.

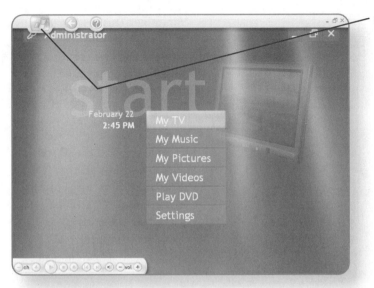

Menu. Regardless of where you are in the Media Center, clicking this button will return you to the main menu.

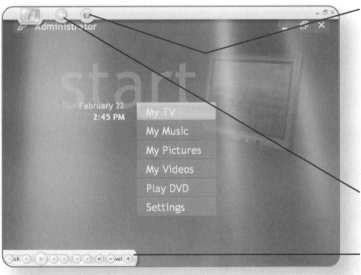

Help. If at any point you are stuck, clicking this button will open a Help window that will provide you with assistance based on the area you are in. For example, if you are in the My Music area and you click the Help button, Help topics related to My Music will appear.

Back. Clicking this button will take you back one screen every time it is clicked.

Controls. Whenever you hover your mouse over any part of the Media Center, a series of controls will appear. These will allow you to control the media you are working with.

- **Minimize**. This button will minimize the Media Center window and will create a button on the taskbar that can be clicked to restore it to its normal size.

- **Maximize/Restore**. Pressing this will expand the Media Center window so that it takes up the entire area of your monitor. If your window is already maximized, pressing this button will restore it to its original size.

- **Close**. Clicking this will close the Media Center and return you to your computer.

2

Watching and Recording Television

America's favorite pastime is now available on your computer! Think of the television functionality of Windows XP Media Center Edition as your regular TV on steroids. Not only can you watch television, you can pause live programming, conduct instant replays, and search for your favorite shows. In addition to all that, there is a built-in recorder that will allow you to record and play back any programs. In this chapter, you'll learn how to:

- Watch television with My TV
- Pause, rewind, fast-forward, and replay TV
- Search for programs
- Record and play back shows

Launching My TV

The television functionality of Windows XP Media Center Edition can be found in the My TV area of the Media Center.

Starting My TV with the Mouse

You can use your mouse to launch the Media Center.

1. Click Start. The Start menu will appear.

2. Click Media Center. The Media Center Window will launch.

3. **Click My TV**. A window with a separate television window will appear.

4. **Click** on the **television window**. The window will now be maximized and television can be viewed as if you were watching a regular TV.

NOTE

With all of the TV functions, you can either use your mouse to click on options or you can use the remote control.

Changing Channels

What's the point of having a television if you are stuck watching only one channel? Windows XP Media Center Edition allows you to scroll through channels or manually enter specific channels.

Scrolling Through Channels

As with most television features, when changing channels, you have the option of using your mouse or the remote control.

1. **Position** the **mouse pointer** over the **television** window. A menu of options will appear in the bottom-left corner of the screen.

2a. **Click** the **+ or − sign**. The + sign will change to the next higher channel while the − sign will move to the next lower channel.

OR

2b. **Press** the **Channel/Page + or – sign** on the remote control to move up or down a channel.

Manually Entering Channels

If you want to quickly jump to a specific channel, you can enter the channel number by using the remote control.

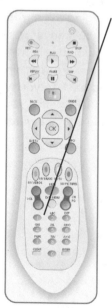

1. **Press** the **number(s)** of the channel you'd like to move to on the remote control.

22 WUTV **Judge Judy** 5:00 PM - 5:30 PM 5:09 PM

As you press the numbers, they will appear in the lower corner of your screen. Several seconds after you enter the number, the channel will change.

Controlling Live Television

It never fails. You're watching your favorite show or the big game, and the phone starts ringing, the baby starts crying, or the vacuum cleaner salesman is ringing at your front door. With Windows XP Media Center, you'll never miss a second of your favorite programming. When you begin watching television with My TV, everything you are watching is being automatically recorded and played back to you with a slight delay. This means that you can actually pause, rewind, replay, and even fast-forward a show while you are watching it.

Pausing Television

Using the remote control or the on-screen menu, you can pause programs as you are watching them. This is possible because Windows XP Media Center automatically records up to 30 minutes of programming and plays it back with a slight delay.

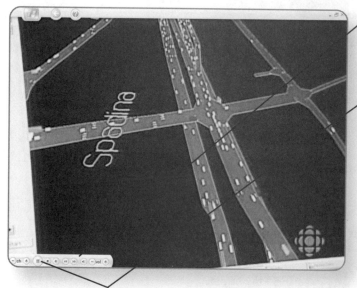

1. **Position** the **mouse pointer** over the **television** window. An on-screen menu will appear in the bottom-left corner of the screen.

2a. **Click** the **Pause** button. The television program will be paused.

OR

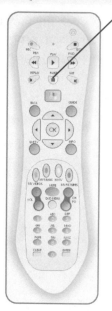

2b. **Press** the **Pause** button on the remote control.

After you've paused a program, the Shifting window will appear, providing you with information.

- **Begin Time.** This represents the point at which the pause began.

- **Pause Time.** Indicates the time at which the program was paused.

- **Recorded Time.** Indicates the point the buffer has recorded to.

Continuing Play

After you've paused a program, you can continue playing the show by pressing Play again.

1a. Click the **Play** button. The television program will begin playing again.

OR

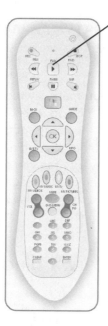

1b. **Press** the **Play** button on the remote control to continue watching the program.

TIP

At any time, you can return to real-time live TV by clicking the Live TV button on your remote control.

NOTE

You cannot use the special TV controls like Rewind and Pause while you are recording a program.

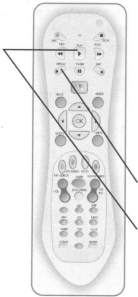

Replay

Windows XP Media Center allows you to be the director of any show that you are watching. Let's say that you are watching your favorite hockey, football, or any other sports team on television. If you want an instant replay of something you just saw, you are no longer at the mercy of the television director. You can instantly replay the last 7 seconds of anything you are watching.

1. **Press** the **Replay** button on the remote control. The program will rewind 7 seconds and pause.

2. **Press** the **Play** button. The program will begin playing from the point it was rewound to.

Rewinding and Fast-Forwarding Programs

The amount of television that is automatically recorded is called the buffer. You can only rewind and fast-forward to the end points of the buffer. Typically, the length of the buffer is a maximum of a half hour from the time you begin watching a certain channel. This means that every time you start to watch a new channel, a new buffer is created. Once again, rewinding and fast-forwarding a program can be controlled using the remote control or the On-Screen menu.

Rewinding and Fast-Forwarding Using the On-Screen Menu

If you prefer using the mouse to control the television, the On-Screen menu provides you with all the tools you need to jump backward or forward in the television program you are watching.

1. **Position** your **mouse pointer** anywhere over the **screen**. The On-Screen menu will appear.

2. **Click** the **Rewind** button. The program will begin rewinding.

As you are rewinding, the Shifting window will appear and will indicate what point you are at in the rewind.

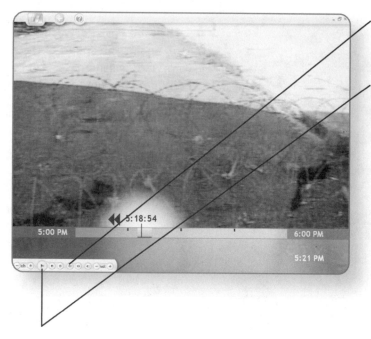

3. **Click** the **Rewind** button **again**. The speed of the rewind will increase.

4. **Click Play**, once you have reached the point where you want to begin viewing.

5. **Click** the **Fast-Forward** button. The program will begin moving forward.

NOTE

You can only use the Fast-Forward function if you have paused or rewound a program.

6. **Click** the **Fast-Forward** button again. The speed of the fast-forward will increase. You can fast-forward until you've reached the point of live programming.

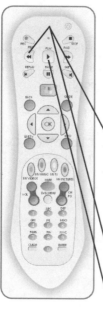

Rewinding and Fast-Forwarding Using the Remote Control

The remote control provides you with an easy way to skip backward or forward in programs without being tied down to your computer.

1. **Press** the **Rewind** button. The program will begin rewinding. You can rewind as far back as the point when the buffer started.

As you are rewinding, the Shifting window will appear and will indicate what point you are at in the rewind.

2. **Press** the **Rewind** button **again**. The speed of the rewind will increase.

3. **Press** the **Play** button, once you have reached the point where you want to begin viewing.

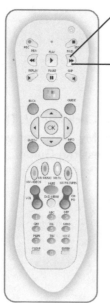

4. **Press** the **Fast-Forward** button. The program will begin moving forward.

5. **Press** the **Fast-Forward** button **again**. The speed of the fast-forward will increase. You can fast-forward until you've reached the point of live programming.

Program Guide

We used to subscribe to the Saturday paper just to get the Television Program Guide, so we'd know what was going to be on TV in the upcoming week. If that's true for you, you can cancel your subscription, because Windows XP Media Center comes with a free interactive Program Guide that will allow you to view what programs are on and get information on the TV listings. The Guide works the same regardless of whether you are using the remote control or the mouse.

Navigating the Guide

You can peruse the different programs in the Guide by using the mouse, or if you prefer, you can follow the same instructions by using the remote control.

1. Click Start. The Start menu will appear.

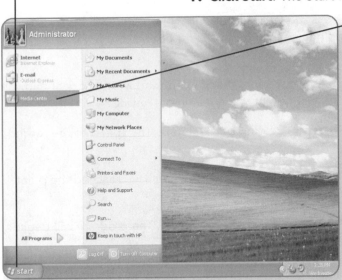

2. Click Media Center. The Media Center screen will appear.

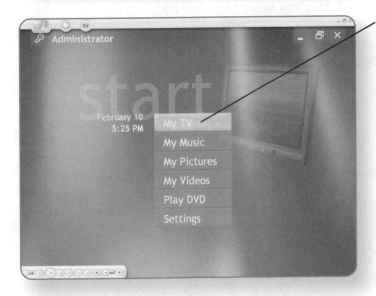

3. Click My TV. This will launch the My TV screen where you can access the Guide.

4. **Click Guide**. The Television Guide will appear.

5. **Position** your **mouse pointer** over a **program**. The program will be highlighted.

Information on the program will appear at the bottom of the page.

6. **Click** on an **arrow** to move up or down channels or backward or forward through show times.

NOTE

The Guide will not display programs in the past; only current or future programs.

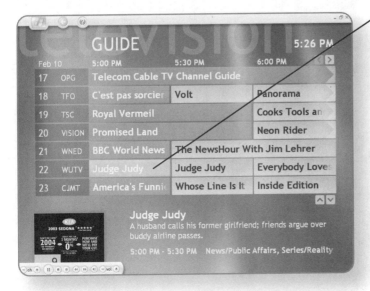

7. **Click** on a **program** that is listed in the left column. Programs in the left-most column are currently playing. The channel will change to the selected channel.

NOTE

The total number of channels that are listed will vary depending on your television provider.

Searching for Programs

When I was a kid, we were excited when our cable went from eight to twenty channels. Nowadays, you can have hundreds of different channels. While the Guide is handy, looking for a particular program can become tedious. To help you, Windows XP Media Center Edition has a built-in search engine that will allow you to find any show, movie, or game that you're looking for.

1. Click My TV in the Media Center window.

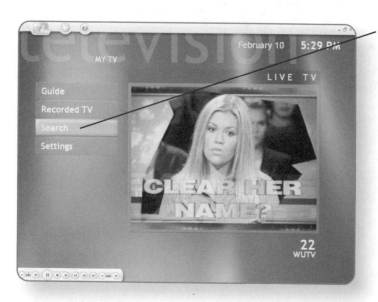

2. Click Search. The Search window will open. You can search by category, title, or a specific keyword.

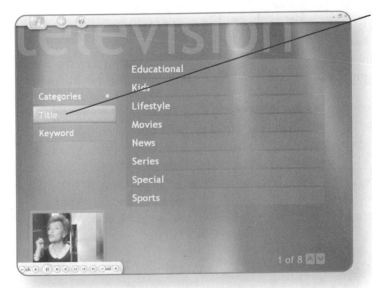

3. **Click Title or Keyword.** You will now be prompted to enter the title or keyword of the program that you are looking for.

4. **Start Typing** the **title or keyword** of the program you are looking for. As you begin typing, results that match your keywords will appear.

5. **Click** on the **desired result**. A list of times and episodes will appear.

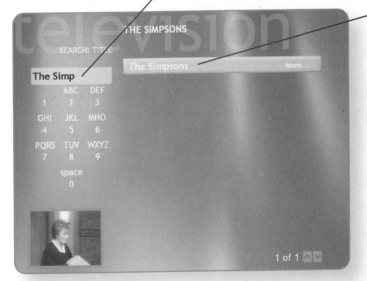

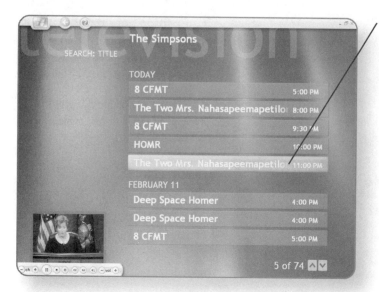

6. Click on the **desired episode**. Information on the episode will appear and options to record the program will be available.

Recording Television

That rectangular box with the flashing lights sitting under or beside your desk is a master of disguise. You'd think by its appearance that it was just a computer, but in fact it also doubles as a VCR. You can record shows, set up scheduled recordings, and replay shows.

Recording a Show That You Are Watching

The easiest way to record a program is to simply click the Record button as you are watching it. All the programs that you record are stored in a central location that can be easily accessed later.

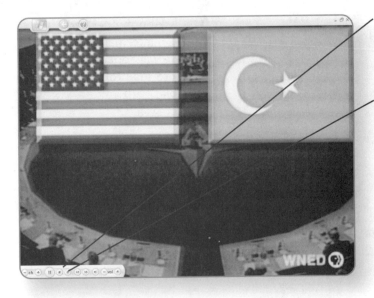

1. **Position** your **mouse pointer** anywhere over the **television** area. The On-Screen menu will appear.

2. **Click** the **Record** button. The program you are watching will be recorded.

A red dot will appear beside the program information at the bottom of the screen to indicate that the program is being recorded. This screen will disappear after several seconds.

3. Position your **mouse pointer** anywhere over the **television** area. The On-Screen menu will appear again.

4. Click the **Stop** button. A dialog box will appear, asking if you are sure that you want to stop the recording.

TIP

If you click Record while watching a program, the Record session will automatically stop at the end of the scheduled program.

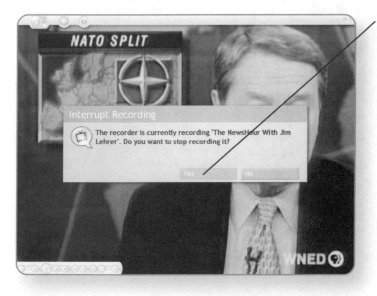

5. Click Yes. The recording will stop.

Recording a Show Using the Guide

Using the Guide, you can find particular programs and set them to be recorded. You can choose to record one episode of the program or the entire series.

1. **Click My TV**. This will launch the My TV screen where you can access the guide.

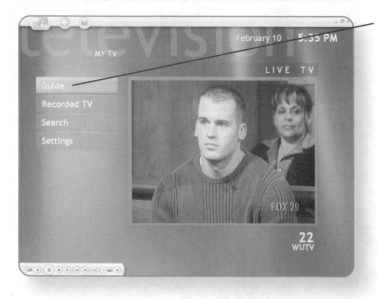

2. **Click Guide**. The Television Guide will appear.

3. **Click** on the **future show** that you would like to record. A Program Information screen will appear.

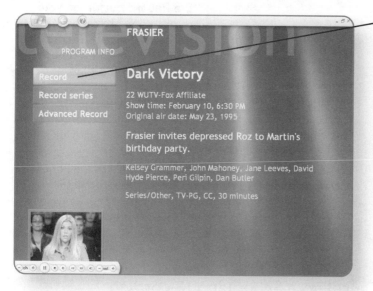

4. **Click Record**. Alternatively, you can select **Record Series**, which will record this program whenever it is on. You will be returned to the Guide.

NOTE

The computer must be on or in standby mode to record a program.

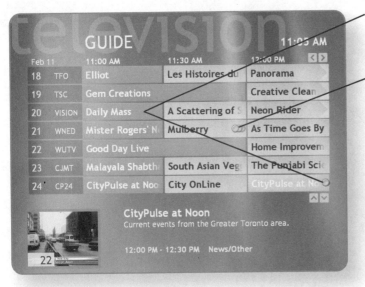

A red dot will appear beside the program to indicate it will be recorded.

A series of red dots indicates that the entire series is set to record.

TIP

Using the Record button on the remote control, you can quickly choose to record a program, record a series, or cancel a recording. While highlighting a program in the Guide, you can click the Record button on your remote once to record the program, twice to record the series, or three times to cancel a recording.

NOTE

Windows XP Media Center Edition can only record one program at any particular time. If there is a conflict in your recording schedule, a screen will appear asking you which of the programs you would like to record.

Canceling a Scheduled Recording

If you've decided that you want to cancel a recording you've scheduled using the Guide, you simply select it and then cancel the recording.

1. **Click** on the **program** that you'd like to cancel in the Guide. A screen will appear where you can cancel the recording.

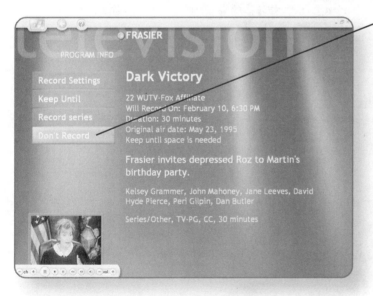

2. **Click Don't Record.** The recording will be canceled.

Manual Recording

Just like a normal VCR, you can schedule recordings by setting a specific date, time, and channel to record.

1. Click Start. The Start menu will appear.

2. Click Media Center. The Media Center will launch.

3. Click Settings. The Settings screen will appear.

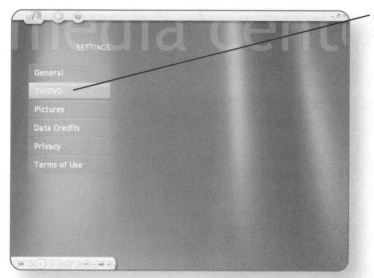

4. Click TV/DVD. More setting options will appear.

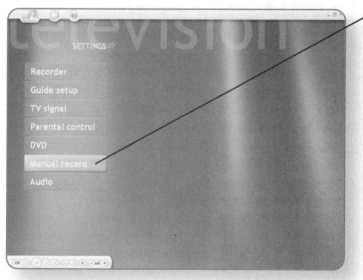

5. Click Manual record. You can now enter the specific recording information.

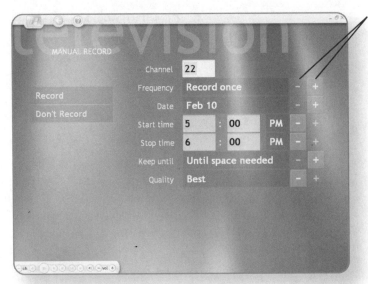

6. Click the **–** or **+** beside each option to adjust it.

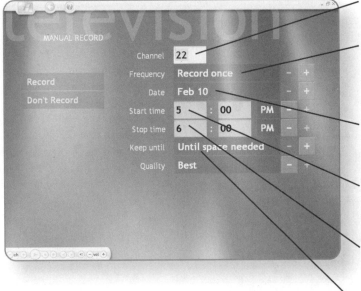

- **Channel.** Select what channel you'd like to record.

- **Frequency.** Here you can determine how often you want this recording to take place.

- **Date.** This indicates when you want the recording to take place.

- **Start time.** Type the time when you want the recording to begin.

- **Stop time.** Type the time when you want the recording to end.

- **Keep until.** This option determines how long the recording is to be kept on your hard drive.

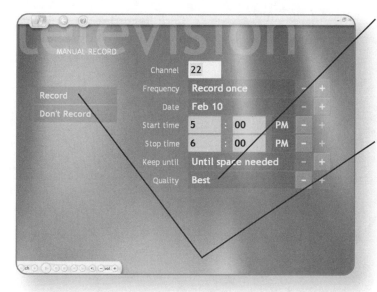

- **Quality.** This will determine the resolution of the show you are recording. The higher the quality, the more space the recording will require on your hard drive.

7. Click Record after you've finished adjusting the options. The settings will take effect and the channel will be recorded at the time you have set.

Watching Recorded Programs

Windows XP Media Center Edition automatically stores and categorizes your programs so that they can be easily found and replayed.

1. Click My TV in the Media Center window.

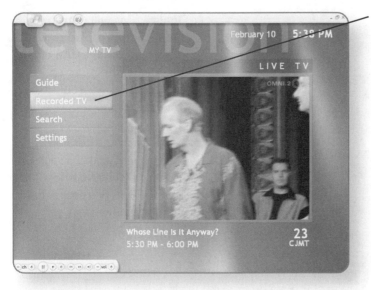

2. **Click Recorded TV**. A list of the programs you've recorded will appear, categorized by date.

3. **Click** on the **Sort** option. The recordings will be sorted based on the option you've selected.

4. **Click** on the **Recording** that you'd like to view. A Program Info Screen will appear giving you information on the recording.

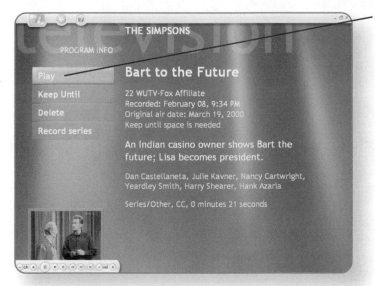

5. **Click Play**. The recording that you have selected will be played. Just like an ordinary VCR, you can fast-forward, rewind, pause, or stop the recording at any time.

NOTE

Windows XP Media Center Edition allows you to back up your recorded programs, but they can only be replayed on the computer that they were recorded on.

3

DVD Player

What do 8-track tapes, platform shoes, beta max, and Cabbage Patch Kids have in common with the VCR? Just like those items, the VCR will soon be a relic of the past. With the rising popularity of DVD, it's no wonder that Windows XP Media Center Edition has a built-in DVD player. In this chapter, you'll learn how to:

- Play DVDs
- Access DVD controls

Playing a DVD

Windows XP Media Center Edition will automatically recognize a DVD when it is inserted into the computer's DVD drive. You will be prompted with a dialog box asking you what you'd like to do with the DVD.

1. Insert the **DVD** into the DVD drive. The DVD will start spinning and a dialog box will open.

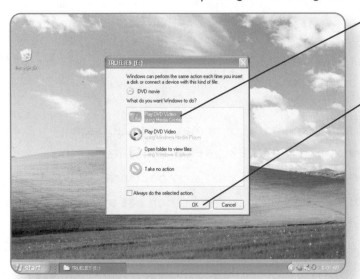

2. Click Play DVD Video using Media Center if it is not already selected. It will be highlighted, once selected.

3. Click OK. The DVD will begin to play.

NOTE

Typically, DVDs have their own Title Screen, which provides you with options to watch special features, jump to different chapters, or simply play the movie. Using your mouse or remote control, you can click or select the desired option from the DVD Title Page.

Depending on how your computer was configured, there is a chance that when you insert the DVD you will not automatically be prompted to play the DVD in Media Center. If you place the DVD in the drive and nothing happens, follow these steps:

1. Click Start. The Start menu will appear.

2. Click Media Center. The Media Center window will open.

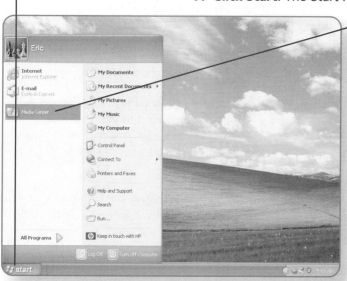

3. Click Play DVD. The DVD will begin playing.

DVD Controls

A DVD can be controlled by either using the On-Screen menu or the buttons on the remote control. Typically, DVDs are divided into different chapters. Using the DVD controls, you jump to different chapters, access the DVD main menu, pause, rewind, fast-forward, and stop the video.

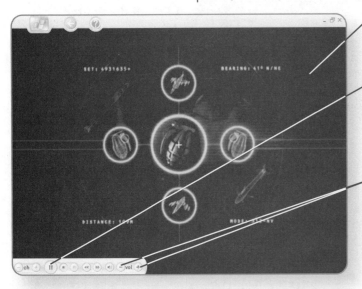

1. Position the **mouse pointer** anywhere over the **window**. The On-Screen menu will appear.

- **Pause/Play.** This button will pause the video. Once paused, it will change into a Play button to allow you to restart the video.

- **Volume.** Clicking the + or – sign will increase or decrease the volume.

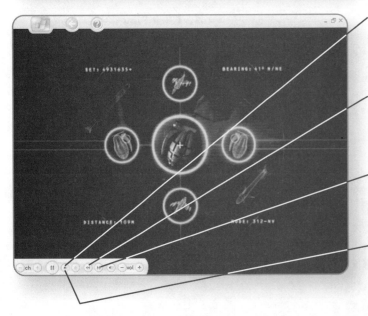

- **Stop.** This button will stop the video and open up a window where you can choose from several options.

- **Rewind.** This will rewind the movie until you reach the beginning or you press the Stop or Play button.

- **Fast-Forward.** This will forward the video until you press the Stop or Play button.

2. Click Stop. A menu will appear, giving you various options.

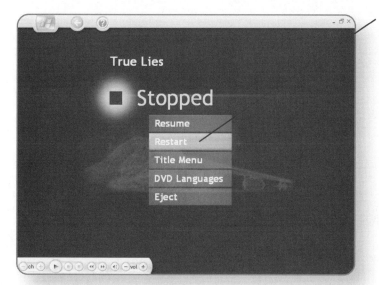

True Lies

■ Stopped

Resume
Restart
Title Menu
DVD Languages
Eject

3. **Click** the **desired option**. Depending on the option you choose, the computer will react accordingly.

TIP

The buttons on your remote control work in the same manner as the On-Screen menu buttons but offer you a little more functionality. Pressing the Replay or Skip buttons will move the video either backward or forward, one chapter at a time.

4

Playing Music

Windows XP Media Center Edition will literally be music to your ears. It supports a wide range of both digital and conventional music formats. This means that you can not only play your CDs, but you can also take advantage of popular digital formats like MP3. In this chapter, you'll learn how to:

- Play CDs
- Create a Music Library
- Digitize music
- Search for music
- Create a Playlist
- Create an Automatic Disc Jockey

Playing a Music CD

Whenever a new technology comes out, it seems like you have to throw away the investment you made in an existing technology. Not the case with your CDs. Not only can you play your CDs on your computer, you can also digitize them and save them in a variety of formats.

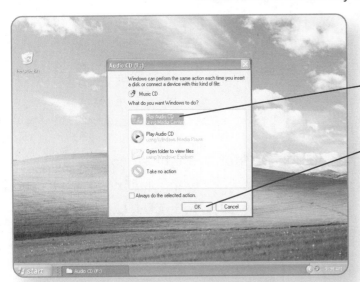

1. Insert the **CD** into the CD drive. It will begin spinning and a dialog box will appear.

2. Click Play Audio CD using Media Center if it is not already selected.

3. Click OK. Media Center will launch and the CD will begin playing.

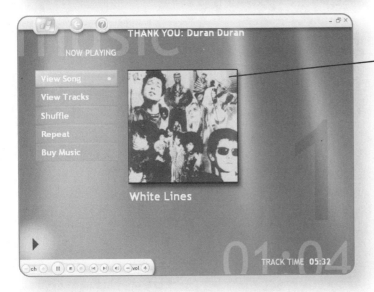

NOTE

A picture of the album and the names of the tracks will only appear if you are connected to the Internet. If you aren't connected, or if the album is independent or not well known, the music files will appear as Unknown and only the track numbers and time will be shown.

Depending on how your computer was configured and what options were previously selected, the dialog box prompting you to start Media Center might not automatically appear. If this is the case, use the following steps:

1. Click Start. The Start menu will appear.

2. Click Media Center. The Media Center window will open.

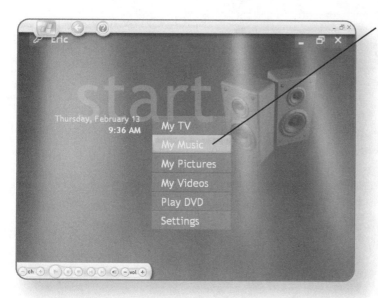

3. Click My Music. A window will open and the album in the CD drive will appear.

4. Double-click on the **album**. It will begin playing, and a list of tracks on the album will appear.

CD Controls

Using the On-Screen menu or the remote control, you can select which tracks to play, pause songs, shuffle play, or repeat songs. When you are connected to the Internet, you can even purchase music through the Media Center.

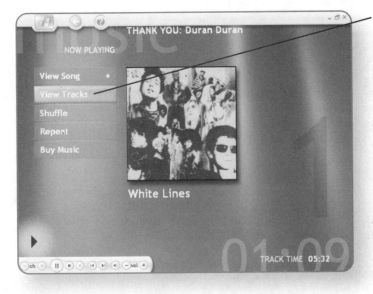

1. Click View Tracks. A list of all of the tracks on the CD will appear.

2. Click once on any **track**. The track will begin playing.

3. Position the **mouse pointer** anywhere over the **Media Center window**. The On-Screen menu will appear.

4. Click the **Forward or Back** button to move forward or back one track at a time.

5. Click Pause to pause the track. Once paused, the button will turn to a Play button, which can be clicked to restart the track.

6. Click Repeat. A check mark will appear in the box. Once the CD has played all of its tracks, it will start at the beginning again while Repeat is selected.

7. Click Shuffle. A check mark will appear in the box. When you click Shuffle, the tracks will be randomly distributed in the playlist.

Windows Media Player

Before you can take advantage of My Music, the music section of the Media Center, you must first find and organize the music on your computer. This can be done through Windows Media Player. Windows Media Player also allows you to create playlists and digitize your existing CD collection.

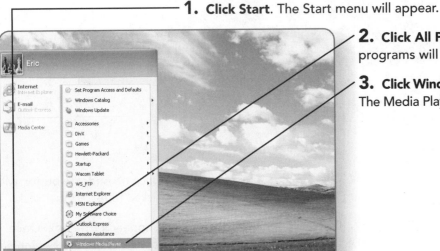

1. Click Start. The Start menu will appear.

2. Click All Programs. A list of programs will appear.

3. Click Windows Media Player. The Media Player will launch.

Creating a Music Library

If you already have music files on your computer, Windows Media Player will automatically search for those files and add them to the library. Once a library is created, the music can later be accessed in the My Music area of the Media Center.

1. **Click Tools**. The Tools menu will appear.

2. **Click Search For Media Files**. A dialog box will open.

3. **Click Search**. A search for the media files on your computer will begin. Depending on the size of your computer's hard drive and the number of files you have, this may take several minutes. Windows Media Player will automatically categorize the music by album, artist, genre, and song.

4. **Click Close,** once the search is complete.

TIP

Rather than searching your computer to add more music files, you can simply copy the files to the My Music folder, which is located in the My Documents folder on your hard drive. For more information on copying and moving files, see the chapter entitled "File Management."

5. **Click Close** to close the dialog box.

6. **Click** the **x** in the top-right corner to close Windows Media Player.

Creating Playlists

Imagine that you ran your own radio station and you could choose any songs you wanted and could control what order they are played in. Playlists in Windows XP Media Center Edition can make your dream of becoming a DJ come true. A playlist is simply a list of songs that you create that indicates what order the songs you've selected should be played in.

1. Click Media Library. The screen will change so that you can now create a playlist.

2. Click New playlist. You will be prompted to give the playlist a name.

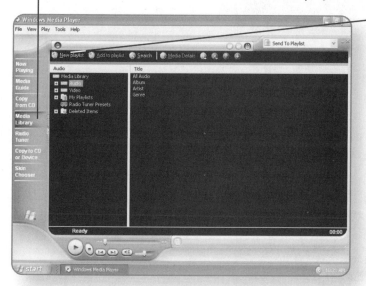

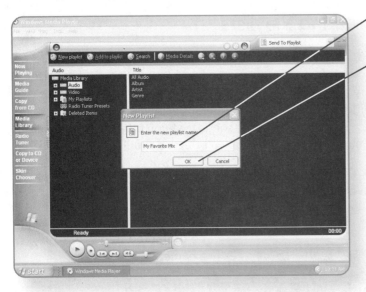

3. **Type** a **name** for the playlist. You can give it any name you like.

4. **Click OK**. The playlist will be created with the name that you chose. You must now add songs to your playlist.

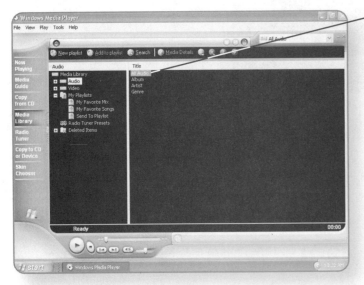

5. **Double-click All Audio**. A list of all of your songs will appear.

6. Click on a **song** that you would like to add to your playlist.

7. Click Add to playlist. A list of the playlists you've created will appear.

8. Click the **desired playlist**. The song you selected will be added to that playlist.

9. **Repeat Steps 6 through 8** until you have added all of the songs to your playlist.

10. **Click** on your **playlist** in the left pane of the window. All of the songs that you have added to your playlist will appear.

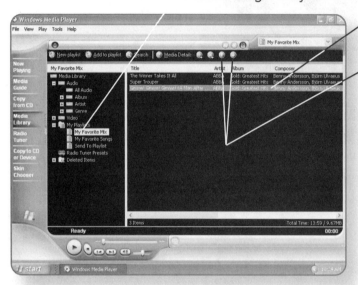

11. **Click** on a **song** that you would like to move.

12. **Click** the **Up or Down arrow** to change where the song appears in the playlist.

Digitizing Songs

You've spent hundreds to thousands of dollars on the CD collection, and now everything has gone digital—what to do? Before you throw out your favorite tunes, take advantage of the functionality of Windows Media Player that will digitize the songs on your CDs and automatically add them to your library.

1. **Insert** the **CD** into the CD drive.

2. **Click Copy from CD**. A list of all of the tracks on the CD will appear.

3. **Click** the **box** beside each song that you would like to digitize. By default, all of the songs are selected. A check mark in the box indicates that it is selected.

4. **Click Copy Music**. The songs that you have selected will be digitized and added to your music library. Depending on the speed of your computer and the number of tracks, the time it takes to complete the copy will vary.

My Music

With the exploding popularity of digital music, there's no question why Windows XP Media Center Edition allows you to sort, play, share, and delete music files. All of this functionality can be found in the My Music area of the Media Center.

1. **Click Start**. The Start menu will appear.

2. **Click Media Center**. The Media Center window will open.

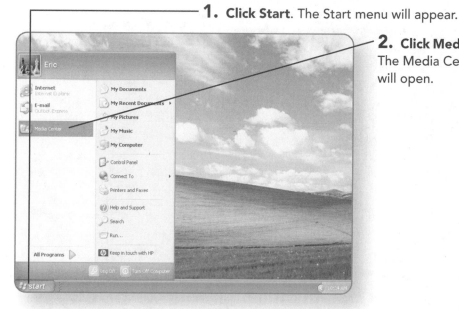

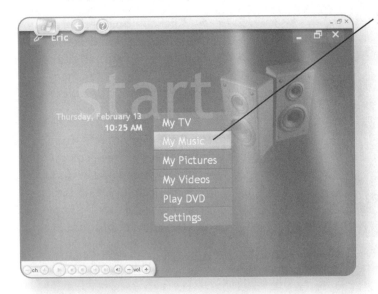

3. **Click My Music**. The My Music window will open and you can view your music.

Playing Music

To play songs in My Music, you simply have to click on the song and it will play.

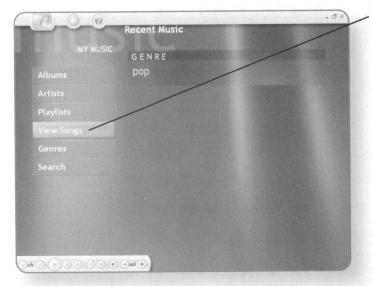

1. **Click View Songs**. A list of all of your songs will appear.

2. Click on the **song** that you'd like to hear. It will begin playing.

3. Position the **mouse pointer** anywhere in the **Media Center window**. The on-screen controls will appear.

4. Click on the **desired control**. Alternatively, you can use the remote control to direct the music.

Searching for Music

It's easy to build up a huge collection of different songs. To help you manage these files, My Music categorizes your music based on albums, artists, playlists, and genres. There is also a built-in search engine that will allow you to quickly find a specific song.

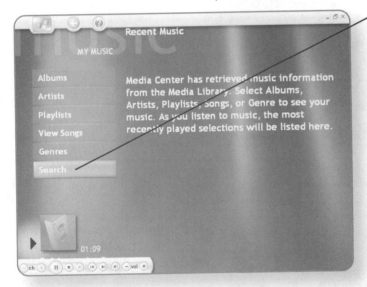

1. Click Search. The Search window will open.

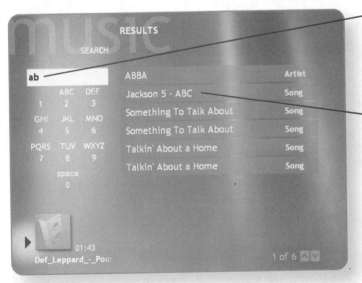

2. Begin typing the **name** of the song or artist that you are searching for. As you type, songs that meet the criteria you've entered will appear.

3. Click on the **desired song**. It will begin playing.

Randomly Playing Songs

One of the categories that the Media Center organizes your music into is genres. A genre is a category of music that fits within a particular style, such as oldies or jazz. When you select a genre, you have the option of randomly playing songs that fall into that genre. That way you can create your own jukebox to listen to particular types of music.

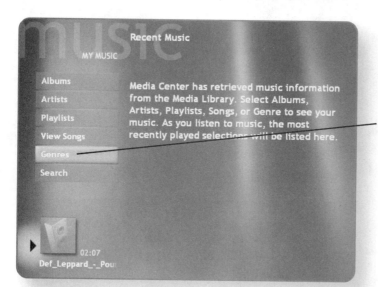

1. Click Genres. A list of genres will appear.

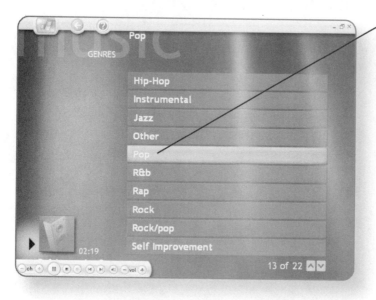

2. Click the **genre** that you would like to listen to. All of the albums that fall within that genre will appear.

3. **Click Shuffle**. All of the songs within that genre will be randomly mixed, and the songs will begin to play.

5

Working with Pictures and Videos

With the decrease in price of digital cameras and scanners, digital photography is becoming a very popular medium. Windows XP Media Center Edition not only allows you to store your digital photos, but you can sort them and create your own slideshows. In this chapter, you'll learn how to:

- Organize your photos
- Sort your photos
- Create and play slideshows

Organizing Your Photos

By default, pictures that you download from cameras or scanners are stored in the My Pictures folder on your computer. If you are adding stored photos from disks or CDs, they should be added into the My Pictures folders. It's a good idea to create separate folders to organize your pictures. For more information on creating folders and copying and moving files, please see the chapter entitled "File Management."

1. **Click Start**. The Start menu will appear.

2. **Click My Pictures**. The My Pictures window will open. A variety of folders and files will appear.

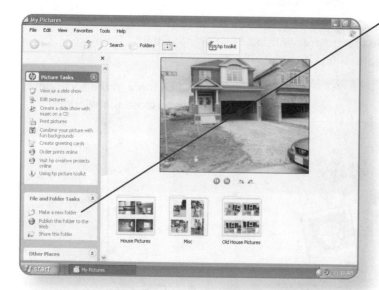

3. Click Make a new folder.
You will now be prompted to
give your folder a new name.

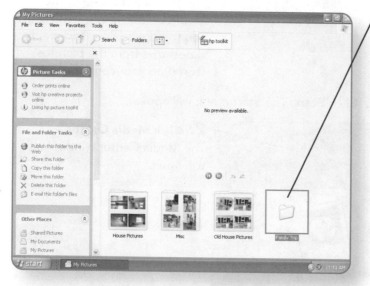

4. Type a **name** for the folder.
The name will appear as you type.

5. Press Enter. The new folder
will be created with the name
that you gave it.

6. Copy any **pictures** you'd like to this new folder. Please see the chapter entitled "File Management" for more information on copying files.

7. Click the **x** in the top-right corner to close the window.

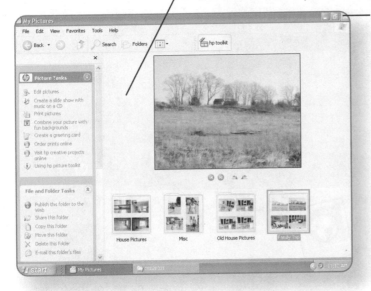

My Pictures

The My Pictures area of the Media Center window will allow you to access, view, and create slideshows from the pictures stored on your computer.

1. Click Start. The Start menu will appear.

2. Click Media Center. The Media Center window will open.

3. Click My Pictures. You will now have access to the pictures on your computer.

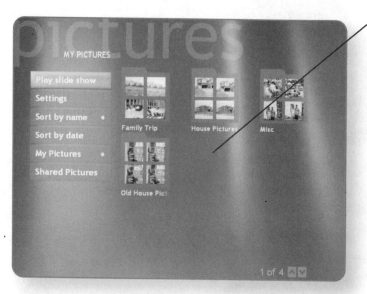

The contents of your My Pictures folder will now be displayed in the window. Both folders and individual picture files will be displayed.

Viewing Pictures

To view pictures, you can simply click on them in the My Pictures window.

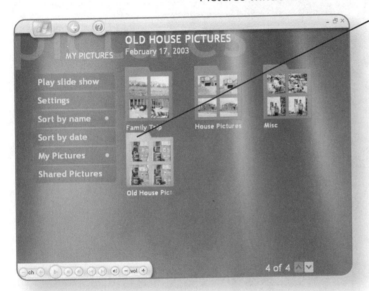

1. Click on the **folder** where the pictures you want to view are stored. The pictures within the folder will be displayed. Alternatively, if you have individual pictures in the My Pictures folder, you can simply click on the picture you'd like to view.

2. Click on the **picture** that you'd like to view. A full-screen preview of the picture will appear.

3. Click the **Back** button. You will be returned to the My Pictures window.

Sorting Pictures

You can organize the pictures in your My Pictures window by name or by date.

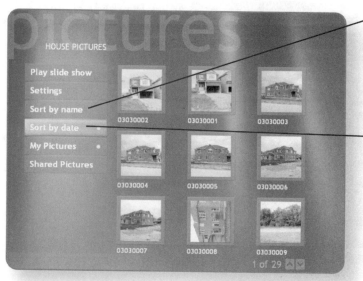

1. Click Sort by name. The pictures and folders will be organized by name. A little dot will appear beside the Sort by name button to indicate that it has been selected.

2. Click Sort by date. The pictures and folders will be sorted by date.

Creating Slideshows

The best way to create a slideshow is to first create a folder that contains all of the photos that you'd like to include in the slideshow.

1. **Click** on the **desired folder** that contains the photos you'd like to have appear in your slideshow.

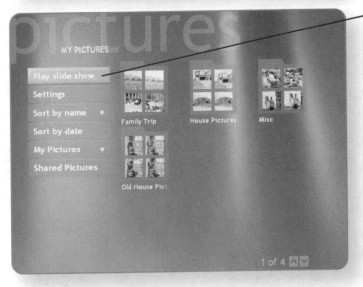

2. **Click Play slide show**. A slideshow of the photos within the selected folder will be displayed.

3. Click the **Back** button to end the slideshow.

TIP

Using the remote control, you can pause the slide-show, advance to slides, or move to previous pictures.

Changing the Slideshow Settings

By adjusting the slideshow settings, you can change the transition time for slides, have pictures appear in random order, or select whether or not pictures in subfolders will appear.

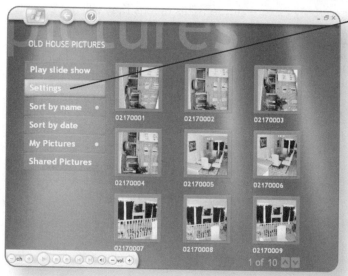

1. Click Settings in the My Pictures window.

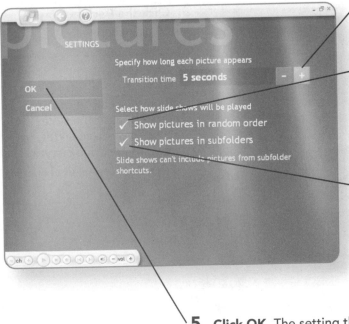

2. **Click the – or + sign** to decrease or increase the transition time between slides.

3. **Click the box beside Show pictures in random order** if you want your slides to appear randomly. A check mark will appear in the box, once selected.

4. **Click the box beside Show pictures in subfolders** if you want pictures in subfolders to be included in your slideshow. The check mark beside the option will indicate whether or not it is selected.

5. **Click OK.** The setting that you chose will be implemented.

Sharing Photos

Every user who has an account set up on your computer has their own My Pictures folder. This means they will not be able to see pictures in your My Pictures folder unless you share them. Once they are shared, anyone who logs onto the computer and goes to the Shared section of the My Pictures window will be able to view those photos.

1. **Click Start.** The Start menu will appear.

2. **Click My Pictures.** The My Pictures window will open.

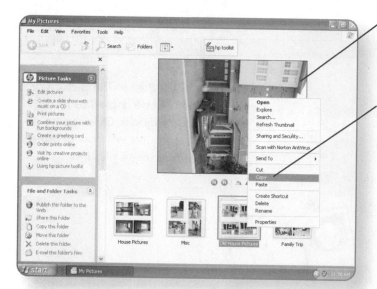

3. Right-click on the **picture** or **folder** that you would like to share with other users on the computer. A menu will appear.

4. Click Copy. The picture or folder will be copied to the clipboard.

5. Click Shared Pictures. The folder containing all of your shared pictures will appear.

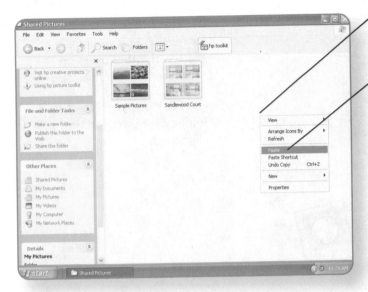

6. Right-click in any **blank area** of the window. A menu will appear.

7. Click Paste. The picture or folder will be copied to the Shared window. Other users on this computer will now be able to access those pictures.

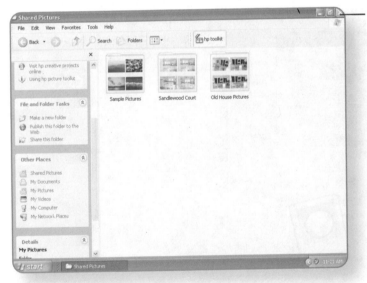

8. Click the **x** in the top-right corner to close the window.

Working with Videos

If you're fortunate enough to own a digital video camera, you can manage and view your videos through the My Videos section of the Media Center. Not unlike managing pictures, you must first place your videos in the My Videos folder.

Managing Video Files

Before you can take advantage of the features of My Videos in the Media Center, you must first copy or move your videos to the My Videos folder.

1. **Click Start**. The Start menu will appear.

2. **Click My Documents**. The My Documents window will open.

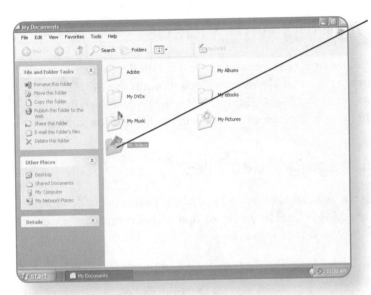

3. Double-click the **My Videos** folder. The My Videos window will open.

4. Copy any **video files** into this folder. For more information on copying or moving files, see the chapter entitled File Management.

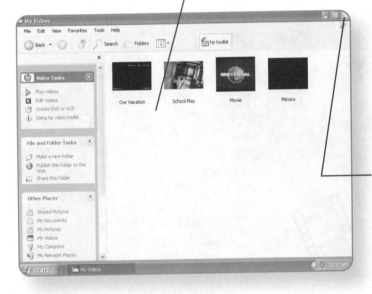

NOTE

Windows XP Media Center Edition supports .asf, .avi, .mpeg, .mpg, .mpe, .mlv, .mp2, .mpv2, .wm, and .wmv video formats.

5. Click the **x** in the top-right corner to close the window, once finished.

My Videos

The My Videos section of the Media Center will allow you to view, sort, and play your video files.

1. **Click Start**. The Start menu will appear.

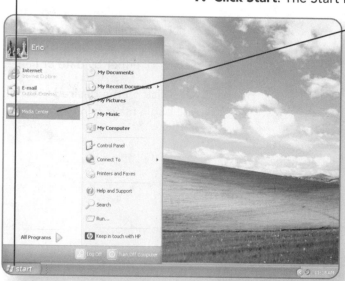

2. **Click Media Center**. The Media Center window will appear.

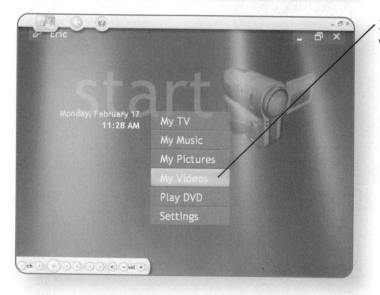

3. **Click My Videos**. The My Videos window will appear.

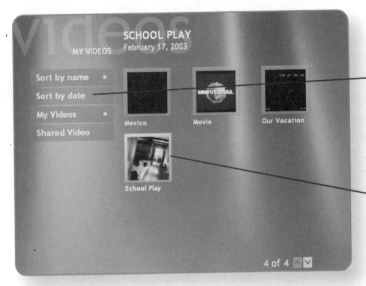

The videos that have been placed in the My Videos folder will appear.

4. Click the **desired Sort by** option. A dot will appear beside the option you've selected. The video files will be rearranged based on the sort option you've selected, either by date or name.

5. Click on the **desired video**. It will begin playing in the window.

6. Click the **Back** button to end the video.

6

The Remote Control

Unlike most computers, your Windows XP Media Center comes with a remote control, which allows you to access all of the multimedia functions that come with your computer. Regardless of who manufactured your computer, all of the remote controls that come with Windows XP Media Center will have similar buttons. Not only can you use the remote control with the Media Center, but you can also use it to navigate throughout your computer instead of using the mouse or keyboard. In this chapter, you'll learn:

- Remote control sections
- Functionality of each remote control button

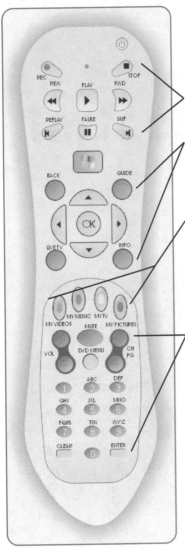

Remote Control Sections

The remote control is divided into four main groups that will allow you to quickly find the buttons that you are looking for.

- **Media Controls.** The buttons in this section allow you to control the playback of your media.

- **Navigation Controls.** Using the buttons in this section, you can navigate around the Media Center. These buttons will also allow you to jump to different windows in the Media Center.

- **Direct Access.** This section of the remote control will allow you to quickly jump to specific types of media, including television, music, pictures, and videos. The buttons in this section also allow you to put the computer in standby mode or browse through television programs that you've recorded earlier.

- **Audio and Video.** With these buttons, you can control the sounds, enter numerical data, and change channels and volume.

NOTE

Not every Windows XP Media Center Edition remote control will look identical. Most will share the common buttons, but they may be located in different places.

Getting to Know the Remote Control Buttons

Each button on the remote control serves its own function. Once you know what a button does, just press it and—voilá—the function will be carried out.

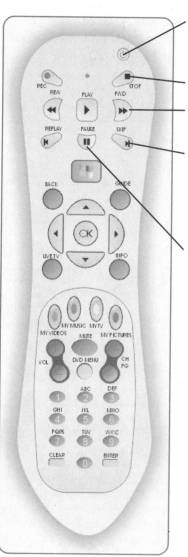

- **Standby.** This will put your computer in standby mode. There is a little light under the Standby button that will flash every time a button is pressed.

- **Stop.** This will stop the media that is playing.

- **Fast-Forward.** Pressing the Fast-Forward button will jump your media forward at three different speeds.

- **Skip.** Pressing the Skip button will jump your media forward. If you are watching videos or live TV, it will jump forward 30 seconds. If you are watching a DVD, it will jump forward one chapter. If you are listening to a music track, it will jump forward one track

- **Pause.** The Pause button will allow you to temporarily pause the media that you are using. Pressing the Pause button again will begin playing the media again.

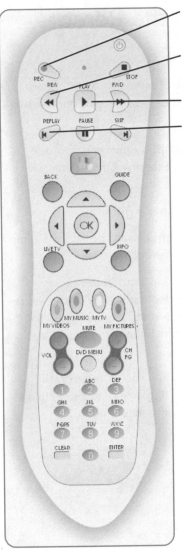

- **Record.** Pressing this button will record the program that you are currently watching.

- **Rewind.** The Rewind button allows you to move the media backward. There are two different rewind speeds.

- **Play.** This will play the media that you have selected.

- **Replay.** Depending on the type of media you are using, the Replay button will replay the last 7 seconds of videos or live TV, it will move back one music track, or it will rewind to the last chapter if you are watching a DVD.

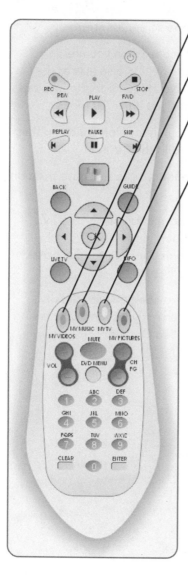

- **My Videos.** Pressing the My Videos button takes you to a screen where you can sort, play, or share videos.

- **My Music.** This will open the Music window so you can play your favorite songs.

- **My TV.** This will open the TV window where you can view the TV Guide, change settings, or search for a particular program.

- **My Pictures.** This button will allow you to navigate through the different images on your computer, sort them, and play them as a slideshow.

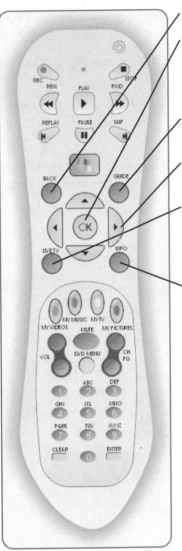

- **Back.** This will take you back one screen or step.

- **OK.** This will select the desired action when you are navigating through the Media Center. OK also acts as the Last Channel button, which will allow you to jump to the previous channel you were watching, when you are in TV mode.

- **Guide.** This button will open your Television Guide so that you can view what's on now and in the future.

- **Arrows.** The Arrows buttons allow you to navigate through the Media Center.

- **Live TV.** If you've paused a program, pressing Live TV will return you to the current point in the live TV program. Pressing Live TV will jump you to the full-screen television mode.

- **Info.** Pressing this button will provide you with details about the media that you are currently viewing or listening to. On some remotes, this is called Details.

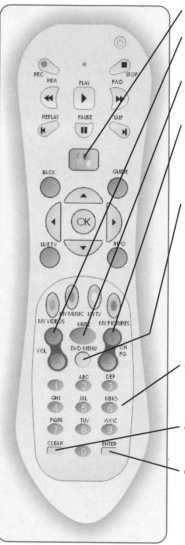

- **Start.** Press this button to open the Media Center.

- **Volume.** These buttons will either increase or decrease the volume.

- **Mute.** This will temporarily turn off the sound until you press the Mute button again.

- **Channel/Page.** These buttons will either change the channels if you are in TV mode or will move the screen up or down a page when you are navigating through the Media Center.

- **DVD Menu.** If you are watching a DVD, this button will open the main menu of the DVD.

- **Numbers.** Pressing different numbers will change the channels when you are in TV mode. The numbers can also be used to enter text in the Media Center.

- **Clear.** If you are entering text or data, the Clear button will take you back one space.

- **Enter.** This button will choose the selected action in the Media Center.

7

Configuring Media Center

The Media Center can be configured and customized after you have completed the First Run Wizard. There are a variety of settings that you can adjust to better control how the Media Center works and keep it up to date. In this chapter, you'll learn how to:

● Update the Program Guide

● Configure the TV Signal

● Set Parental Controls

● Adjust Recorder Settings

● Add programs to the Media Center menu

Updating the Program Guide

The Program Guide that was selected when you first set up Media Center can be altered to include or exclude certain channels, and it can be updated to reflect changes in programming.

Hiding Channels

Most people don't have access to every channel that their cable provider carries. The Guide can be customized to include or exclude channels that you may or may not receive with your cable package.

1. **Click Start**. The Start menu will appear.

2. **Click Media Center**. The Media Center window will open.

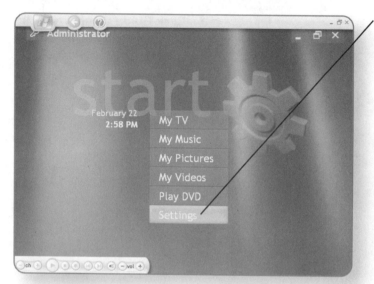

3. Click Settings. A list of Settings categories will appear.

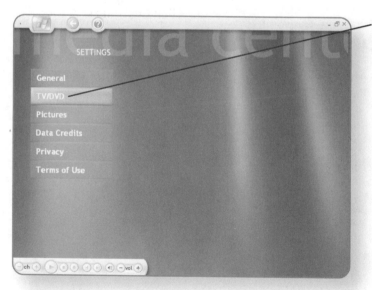

4. Click TV/DVD. You will now be able to select which option to change.

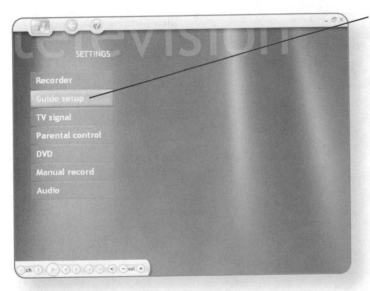

5. **Click Guide setup**. This will open a screen where you can manipulate the Guide data.

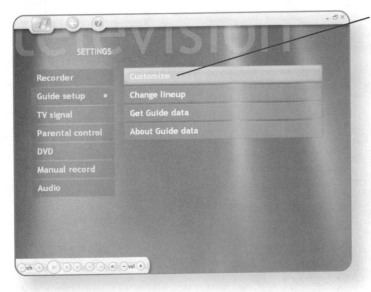

6. **Click Customize**. A window will appear with all of your channels.

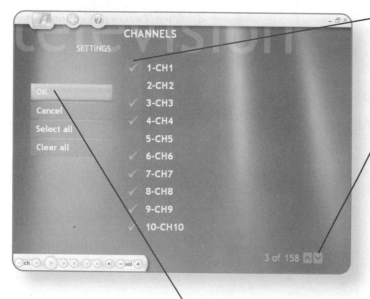

7. **Click** on the **check mark** beside a program to deselect it. Programs with a check mark beside them will appear in the Guide while those without a check mark will not appear in the Guide.

8. **Click** the **up or down arrows** to scroll through the channels, and continue selecting or deselecting channels.

9. **Click OK,** once you have completed selecting or deselecting channels to be displayed.

Updating the Program Guide

From time to time, Windows XP Media Center Edition will automatically update the Guide to reflect changes and keep up to date with programming. You can complete this task manually through the settings.

NOTE

You must be connected to the Internet in order to update the Guide.

1. **Click Settings.** The Settings menu will appear.

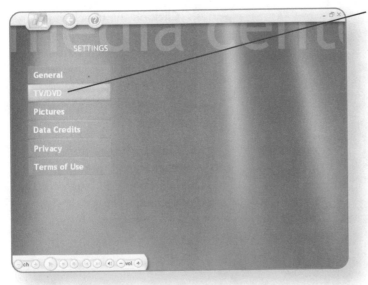

2. Click TV/DVD. Options for your TV will now appear.

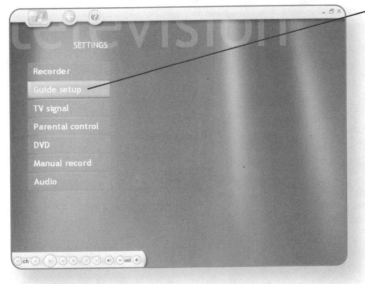

3. Click Guide setup. The screen will change so that you can change Guide options.

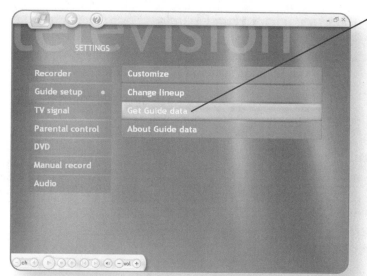

4. Click **Get Guide data**.
A dialog box will now appear, asking if you want to download the Guide data.

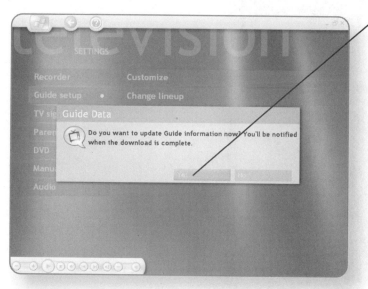

5. Click **Yes**. The Guide will be updated.

Reconfiguring the Guide

Once you've run the First Run Wizard, you can always go back and change the settings selected for the Guide.

1. **Click Settings**. The Settings menu will appear.

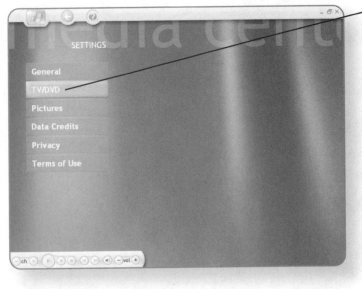

2. **Click TV/DVD**. Options for your TV will now appear.

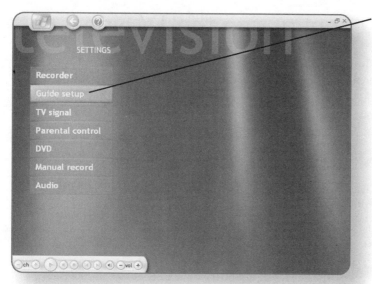

3. **Click Guide setup.**
The screen will change so that you can change Guide options.

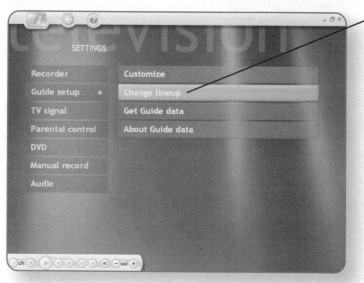

4. **Click Change lineup.**
A wizard will now launch, taking you through the configuration process. Continue following the wizard until you've entered all the requested information.

Reconfiguring the TV Signal

When you first set up the Media Center, you were taken through a wizard that allowed you to enter information on your TV Signal. You can alter any information that you entered about your TV Signal through the settings.

1. Click Settings. The Settings menu will appear.

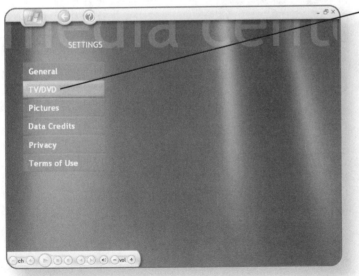

2. Click TV/DVD. Options for your TV will now appear.

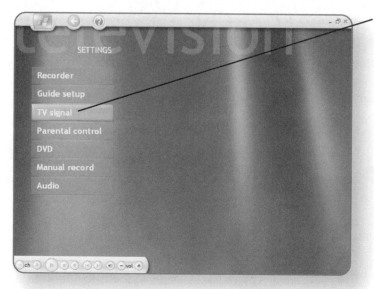

SETTINGS

Recorder
Guide setup
TV signal
Parental control
DVD
Manual record
Audio

3. Click TV signal. A wizard will now launch, taking you step by step through the process of setting up your TV Signal.

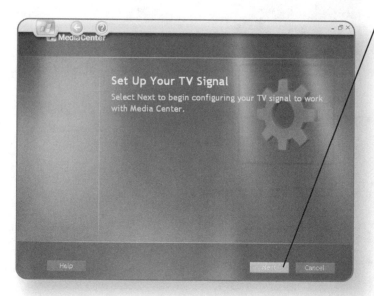

MediaCenter

Set Up Your TV Signal

Select Next to begin configuring your TV signal to work with Media Center.

Help   Next   Cancel

4. Click Next to begin the wizard. Follow the steps of the wizard until all the requested information has been entered.

Parental Controls

Windows XP Media Center Edition provides you with the ability to block channels or programs that are rated at a certain level that you might deem inappropriate for children to watch. The Parental Controls will require that a 4-digit PIN be entered every time a blocked channel is selected.

1. Click Settings. The Settings screen will appear.

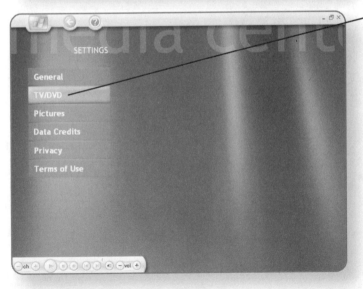

2. Click TV/DVD. Options for your TV settings will appear.

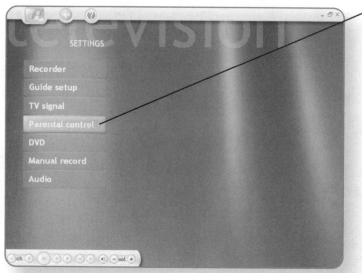

3. **Click Parental control**.
You will now be asked to enter a
4-digit PIN number.

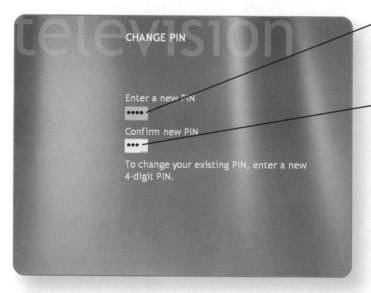

4. **Type** a **4-digit PIN**. It will
appear as a series of asterisks so
nobody watching the screen will
be able to see the PIN.

5. **Retype** the **4-digit PIN** to
confirm it was entered properly.
As soon as you reenter the PIN,
you will be advanced to the next
screen.

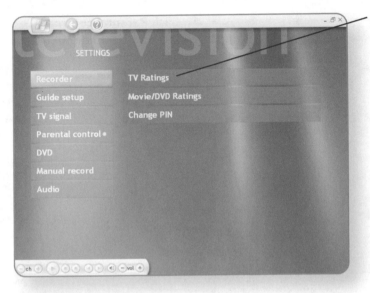

6. Click TV Ratings. You will now be prompted to select what rating level you would like to block.

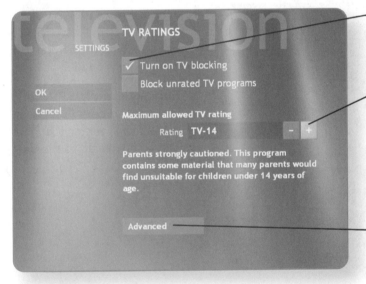

7. Click the **box** beside **Turn on TV blocking.** A check mark will appear in the box, once it is selected.

8. Click the **+ or –** to toggle between the Maximum allowed TV rating. When you turn to a channel that is playing a show that is higher than this rating, you will be prompted to enter the PIN.

9. Click Advanced. The next screen will give you options where you can set restrictive ratings for specific content.

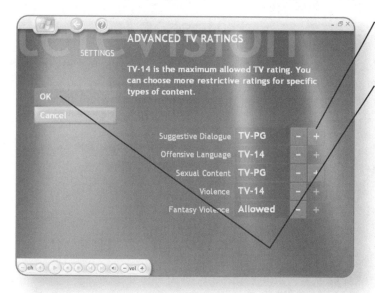

10. **Click** the **+ or –** to toggle between different maximum rating levels for specific content.

11. **Click OK**, once you have completed setting the ratings levels.

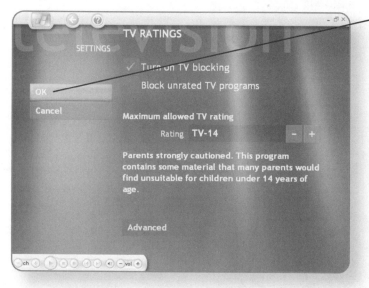

12. **Click OK** to finalize the settings.

Recorder Settings

When you record television programs, there are a variety of options that determine how these programs will be stored. You can control the quality, size, and location of the recordings. These options can be adjusted in the Settings area.

1. **Click Settings**. The Settings screen will appear.

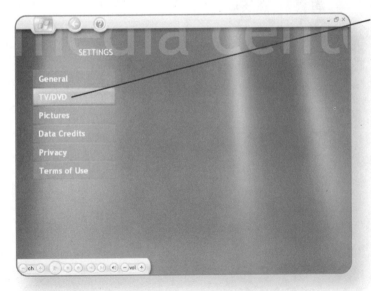

2. **Click TV/DVD**. Options for your TV settings will appear.

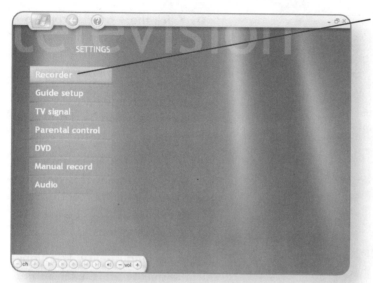

3. **Click Recorder.** A screen of setting options will appear.

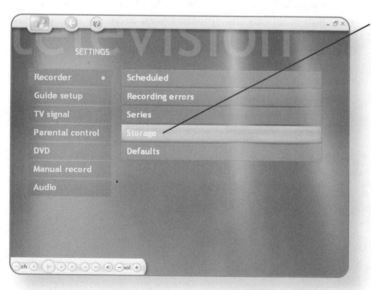

4. **Click Storage.** You can now change how the files will be stored.

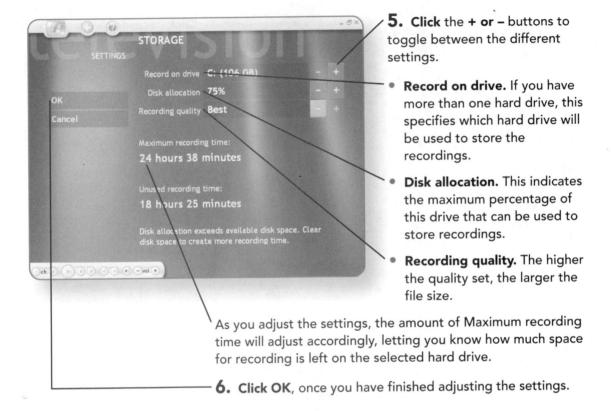

5. **Click** the **+ or –** buttons to toggle between the different settings.

- **Record on drive.** If you have more than one hard drive, this specifies which hard drive will be used to store the recordings.

- **Disk allocation.** This indicates the maximum percentage of this drive that can be used to store recordings.

- **Recording quality.** The higher the quality set, the larger the file size.

As you adjust the settings, the amount of Maximum recording time will adjust accordingly, letting you know how much space for recording is left on the selected hard drive.

6. **Click OK**, once you have finished adjusting the settings.

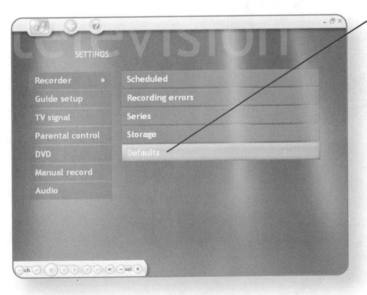

7. **Click Defaults**. A screen will appear where you can adjust the Defaults settings for recording programs.

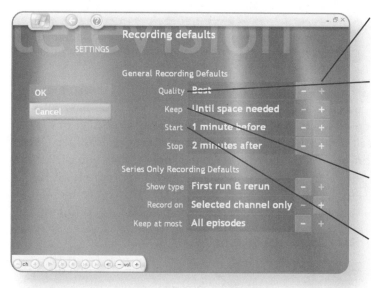

8. Click the **+ or –** to toggle between the different setting options.

- **Quality.** This allows you to change the quality of the recording which, in turn, changes the size of the recorded file.

- **Keep.** You can determine how long a recording is kept by using this option.

- **Start.** As the start time for some programs may be out of sync with the times that are listed in the Guide, you can add a buffer at the beginning of the program to make sure that the program is properly recorded.

- **Stop.** This will add a buffer to the end of the recording.

- **Show type.** When conducting scheduled recordings of a series, you can set this option to record only first-run programs or both first runs and reruns.

- **Record on.** If you have selected to record an entire series, this option allows you to select whether you want the show recorded on any channel that it appears or only on a specific channel.

- **Keep at most.** When recording a series, you can use this option to select how many of the episodes you'd like to keep at any given time.

9. Click OK, once the options have been set.

Adding Programs to the Media Center Menu

The main menu of the Media Center (say that three times fast) is customizable in that you can add links to programs onto the menu. To accomplish this, you must copy a shortcut of the desired program to the Media Center Programs folder. Once a program is on the Media Center menu, when you click that program, Media Center will close and that program will run. In this example, we will add the program "Hearts" to the Media Center menu, but you can do the same with any program.

1. Click Start. The Start menu will appear.

2. Click Run. The Run dialog box will appear.

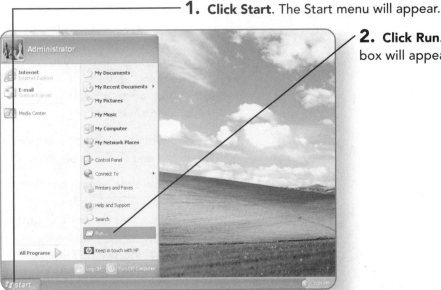

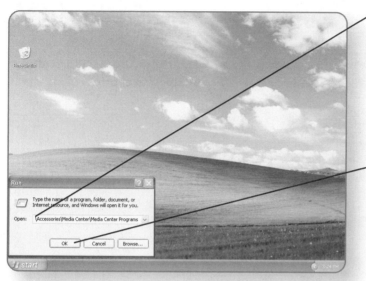

3. Type in **C:\Documents and Settings\All Users\Start Menu\Programs\Accessories\Media Center\Media Center Programs**. This is assuming that Windows XP was installed on your C drive. If not, replace the C:\ with the appropriate drive name.

4. Click **OK**. A window will open showing the empty contents of the Media Center Programs folder.

5. Click **Start**. The Start menu will appear.

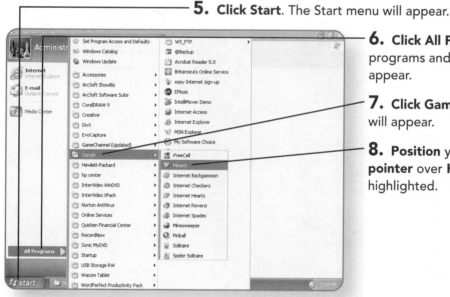

6. Click **All Programs**. A list of programs and categories will appear.

7. Click **Games**. A list of games will appear.

8. **Position** your **mouse pointer** over **Hearts**. It will be highlighted.

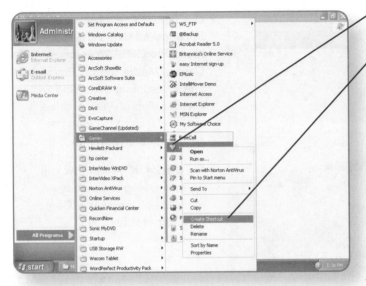

9. **Right-click** on **Hearts**. A menu will appear.

10. **Click Create Shortcut**. A duplicate shortcut of Hearts called Hearts (2) will be made.

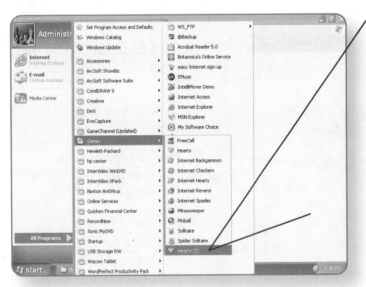

11. **Click** and **drag** the duplicate **Hearts (2)** shortcut to the open window in the background.

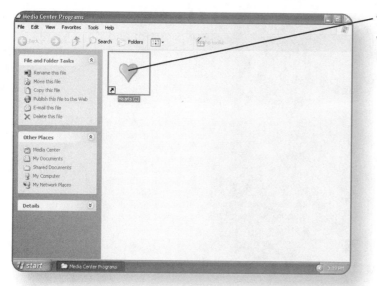

The duplicate Hearts (2) shortcut will now be in the Media Center Programs folder.

12. **Click Start**. The Start menu will appear.

13. **Click Media Center**. The Media Center window will open.

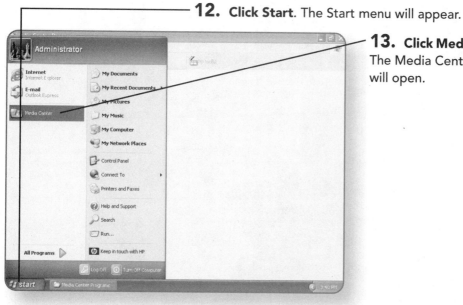

14. **Click Hearts (2)** to launch the program and close Media Center.

8

Windows XP Basics

We need to walk before we run, so if you are new to computers, this is the place to start. After you've set up the multimedia aspects of your Windows XP Media Center computer, it's time to start discovering the world of computing. In this chapter, you'll learn how to:

- Navigate around your computer
- Start programs
- Work with window elements
- End computing sessions

Getting to Know the User Interface

When you start your computer, what you are looking at is the User Interface. The User Interface of Windows XP Media Center is made up of several components:

- **Desktop.** This is the background area of your computer. Everything that you do on your computer is done on top of the desktop.

- **Icons.** Icons are little pictures that represent programs, files, or folders. When you first start Windows XP Media Center Edition, the desktop will have a background image with only one icon on it, the Recycle Bin.

- **Taskbar.** The Taskbar contains the Start button and the Notification tray, and it is used to switch between programs.

- **Start button.** The Start button gives you access to all of the programs and settings on your computer.

- **Quick Launch Bar.** The Quick Launch Bar gives you access to programs with a single click of the mouse button.

- **Notification area.** Located at the right end of the Taskbar, the Notification area contains the clock and will temporarily display icons representing certain tasks.

Starting Programs

There are a variety of different ways that you can start programs in Windows XP Media Center Edition, including using the Start menu, accessing programs through icons, using the Run command, or starting applications using the Quick Launch Bar.

Starting a Program with the Start Menu

The Start button gives you access to everything on your computer. Think of it as the launch pad for everything that you'd like to accomplish with your computer. The Start menu includes both categories of programs and individual programs. In the next chapter, you'll learn to customize the Start menu.

1. **Click** the **Start** button. The Start menu will appear.

2. **Click All Programs**. A list of different programs and categories will appear.

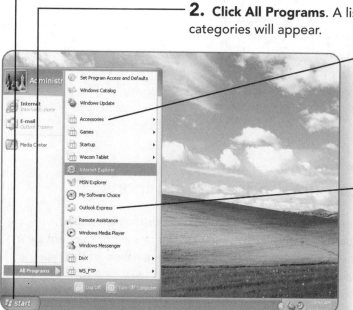

- **Categories.** Categories of programs are represented by an icon, and they have a little arrow indicating that there are programs or subcategories within that category.

- **Individual programs.** Clicking an icon for an individual application will launch that program.

> ### NOTE
>
> The programs installed on your computer may appear different from the ones you see in these images. Each manufacturer installs different programs and configures settings differently when they assemble your Windows XP Media Center computer. That being said, all of the core Windows XP Media Center programs should be the same.

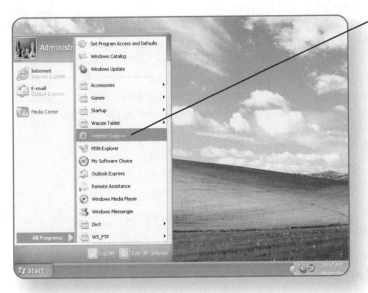

3. Click Internet Explorer. The application will launch. We used Internet Explorer in this example, but you can choose any program.

Starting Programs with Icons

When Windows XP Media Center Edition is installed, depending on the manufacturer, there may or may not be a variety of icons on your desktop. Regardless of the manufacturer, there will always be at least one icon on your desktop: the Recycle Bin. In the next chapter, you will learn how to create a desktop icon for any application. Once you have created an icon, it can be used to launch a program.

1. Position the **mouse pointer** over the icon of the program you'd like to launch.

2. Double-click on the **icon**. This will launch the application that is associated with this icon.

Starting an Application Using the Quick Launch Bar

The Quick Launch Bar is an optional toolbar that fits within the Taskbar. The Program icons that you can add to the Quick Launch Bar are similar to those that you can add to the desktop. The benefit of the Quick Launch Bar is that it allows you to access programs regardless of what other programs you have running. When you have an application open, it typically covers up your desktop, so if you wanted to click on an icon that was on your desktop, you would have to either minimize or close the program you were running. The Quick Launch Bar is never covered, so no matter how many programs you have open, you can quickly launch an application whose icon appears on the Quick Launch Bar. In the next chapter, you'll learn how to add icons to your Quick Launch Bar.

1. **Click** once on an **icon** in the Quick Launch Bar. The application will open.

Starting Programs with the Run Command

Every program that you run is started by a Launch command. In most cases, you wouldn't see or know what the Launch command is, you just click on an icon and let Windows worry about the rest. If you happen to know a Run command, you can start a program using the Run feature. The Run feature will allow you to open a program, a file, a folder, or an Internet resource.

1. **Click** on the **Start** button. The Start menu will appear.

2. **Click Run**. The Run dialog box will open.

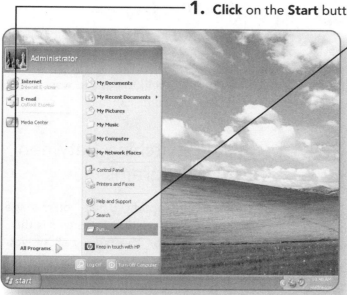

3. **Type** in the **Run command**.

4. **Click OK**. The command will be executed and the program, file, folder, or Internet resource will open.

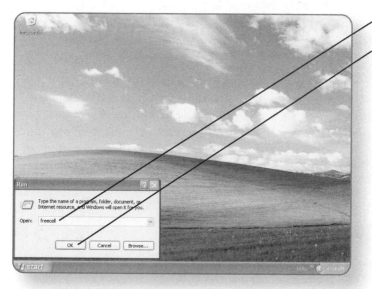

Working with Windows

Whenever a program is launched, it appears in a frame called a window. Because Windows XP Media Center Edition allows you to open up as many different windows as you want, being able to manage open windows becomes an important task.

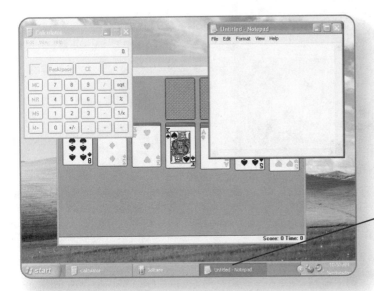

Switching Between Programs

One option to help you manage these multiple programs is the Taskbar. The Taskbar allows you to toggle between the different programs that you have open. Every program that is running is represented by a little Application icon on the Taskbar. There is a button on the Taskbar for each open application.

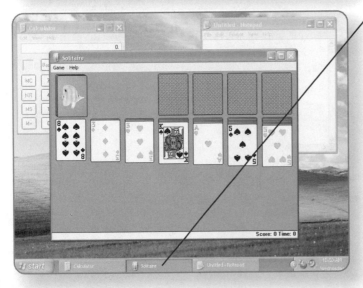

1. Click on the **icon** representing a program in the Taskbar. This will bring the program up in front of all other programs that you are running.

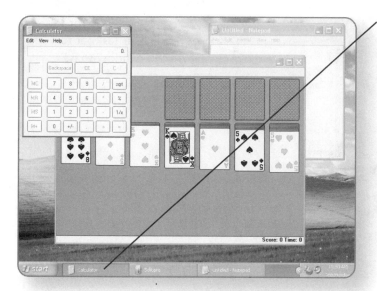

2. Click on another **icon** in the Taskbar. The new program that you have selected will now appear in front of your previous section.

Minimizing and Restoring a Program

There are often times when you'll want to temporarily get a program out of your way so that you can launch another or perform some other task. If you want to get a program out of your way without actually closing it, it can be minimized. Minimizing a program simply means that you are tucking it away temporarily. The program itself won't be affected by being minimized.

1. Click on the **Minimize** button. The window will no longer appear on the screen, but it can still be seen in the Taskbar.

2. Click on the **icon** for the program in the Taskbar to restore the window to its previous state.

Resizing a Window

There may be times when you want to change the size of a Program window so that you can either view more than one program at a time or access the desktop.

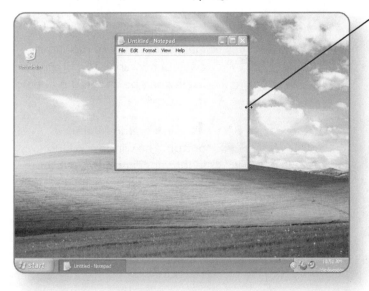

1. Position your **mouse pointer** over the edge of a window. The cursor will change into a double-sided arrow when you are over the correct spot.

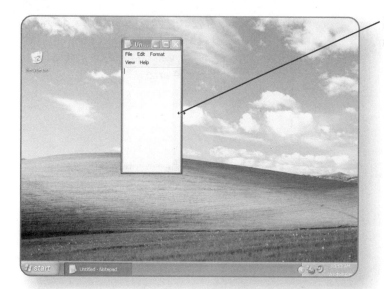

2. **Click** and **drag inward** to reduce the size of the window.

3. **Click** and **drag outward** to increase the size of the window.

4. **Position** the **mouse pointer** in the **bottom-right corner**. The cursor will change to a diagonal double arrow.

5. **Click** and **drag inward** or **outward** to resize the window.

Maximizing and Restoring a Window

If you want your window to take up as much room on the screen as it can, then the Maximize button can be used.

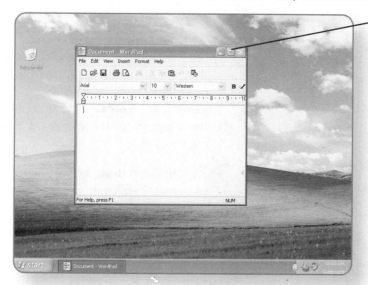

1. **Click** the **Maximize** button. This will make the program as big as it can be on your screen.

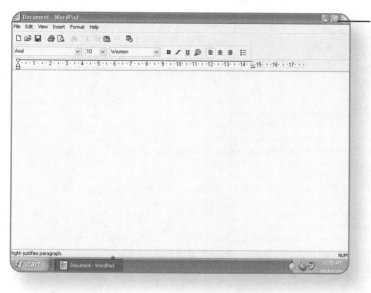

2. **Click** the **Restore** button. This will return the window to its previous size.

Moving a Window

You can easily change the location of a window and reposition it anywhere on your screen. This can be done on any window, except one that has been maximized.

1. Position your **cursor** over the **title bar** area of the window. The title bar is the bar at the top of a window, which is aptly named, as it contains the title of the program or document you are running.

2. Click and **drag** the window to the desired location.

3. Release the **mouse button** and your window will be repositioned.

Scrolling

There will be many occasions when there is more to see in the window than what is currently displayed. Windows XP Media Center Edition provides you with scroll bars that allow you to quickly navigate around your page.

A window can be scrolled through horizontally or vertically, depending on how the information on your page is displayed. Each scroll bar is made up of a scroll box and either an up and down arrow for the vertical scroll bar or a left and right arrow for the horizontal scroll bar. Regardless of whether you are using the vertical or horizontal scroll bar, they both work in the same way.

1. Click on the **down arrow** to scroll down. Each time you click on an arrow, the page will move one line down. Alternatively, you can click on the up arrow to scroll upward.

2. Click and **drag** on the scroll box. The screen will move as you are dragging.

3. Release the **mouse button**. This will allow you to quickly jump to an area.

4. Click anywhere along the **scroll bar**. This will make the window jump to a location between where you clicked and its current location.

Working with Menus

Windows XP Media Center Edition makes your computing experience easier by creating uniformity across applications. Every program that you run will have a certain number of similarities. Almost all programs have a menu bar with a few standard menu items including File, Edit, and Help. The menu bar, which is typically found under the title bar, will give you access to many of the commands within a program. In other words, from the menu bar you can tell a program what to do.

Selecting Menu Items with the Mouse

With your mouse, you can quickly access menu items.

1. **Click** on a **menu** item. A menu will open giving you several options.

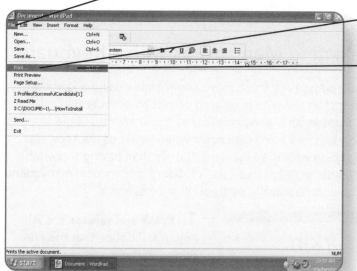

2. **Move** the **mouse** to the desired menu option.

3. **Click** on the desired **option**. Once you click on the option, the command will be executed.

Mouse Shortcuts

Many programs allow you to bring up a special menu by using the mouse. Typically, this menu includes common tasks for that particular program.

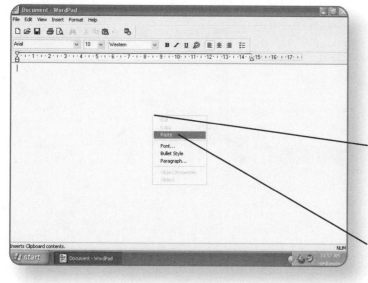

1. **Right-click** in a blank area of your screen. Depending on the application you are running, a menu will now appear where you have clicked.

2. **Click** on the **desired choice**. This will execute the command that you have selected and the menu will then disappear.

TIP

Once you have a menu open, you can click in any blank area of your window to deselect it. Alternatively, you can press the Esc key on your keyboard.

Selecting Menu Items with a Keyboard

Some people are much more comfortable using a keyboard rather than the mouse when it comes to executing commands. This is especially true if you are creating a document in a word processor where most of the time you are typing with the keyboard. Rather than having to switch back and forth between the keyboard and mouse, many menu commands are available through the keyboard.

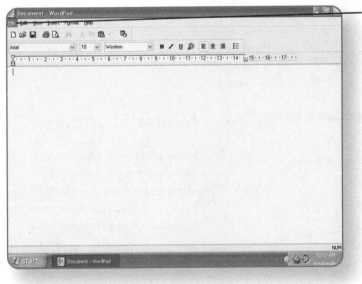

1. Press and **release** the **Alt** key. You'll notice that the File option in the menu bar is highlighted.

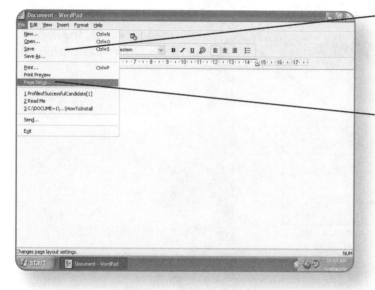

2. **Press** and **release** the **down arrow**. This will expand the File menu. Alternatively, you can press the right or left arrow key to move across the menu bar.

3. **Press** the **down arrow** until you've reached your desired option.

4. **Press** the **Enter** key. This will select your option.

If you take a close look at the menu bar, the menu items across the top all have one letter underlined. Also, each option under every menu item has a letter that is underlined. These letters can be used to quickly jump to menus and execute specific commands.

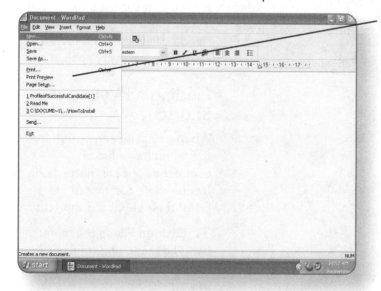

1. **Press** the **Alt** key and the **F** key **at the same time**. This will open the File menu.

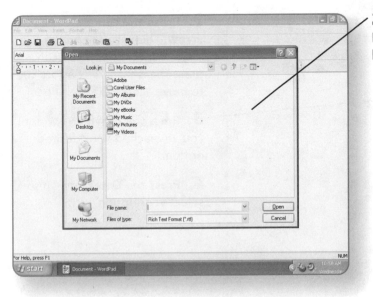

2. Click on the **letter O**. In most applications, this will launch the Open dialog box.

Keyboard Shortcuts

Now that you've learned the long way to work with the menu bar, you'll now learn some tricks for getting your work done even faster. Rather than having to sift through the menus to execute certain commands, there are a variety of keyboard shortcuts that will allow you to instantly perform a task. There are a number of standard keyboard shortcuts that work in almost every application.

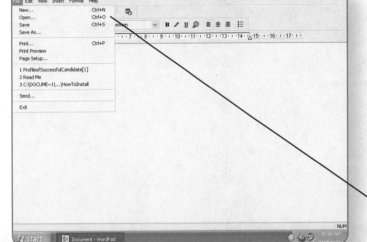

Finding a Keyboard Shortcut

When you select an option from the menu bar, a list of commands appear in the menu. Beside most commands are listed their keyboard shortcuts.

1. Click on **File** in the menu bar. The menu under File will appear. Notice that there is a list of keyboard shortcuts beside many of the commands.

Common Keyboard Shortcuts

To make life a little easier for you, you don't have to learn a whole new set of keyboard shortcuts for every program that you use. For most common functions, there are standard keyboard shortcuts that will work across almost every application in Windows. Table 8.1 lists many of these common shortcuts.

Table 8.1 Keyboard Shortcuts

Keystroke Combination	Name	Description
Ctrl+S	Save	This will save the document that you are working with.
Ctrl+C	Copy	This will copy anything that you have highlighted or selected with your mouse or keyboard.
Ctrl+V	Paste	This will paste anything that you have cut or copied.
Ctrl+X	Cut	This will cut anything that you have highlighted or selected with your mouse or keyboard.
Ctrl+Esc	Launch	This will start the Launch menu no matter what application you are working in.
Ctrl+Alt+Backspace	Restart	This will shut down and restart Windows.
Alt+Tab	Toggle	This allows you to toggle between open programs.
Alt+F4	Quit	This will quit any program that you are working in.
Shift+F1	What's This?	This will turn your cursor into a question mark. It will give a description (if available) of the next thing that you click.
F1	Help	This will open the Help files of many applications.

Special Menu Commands

In working with the menu bar, you may have noticed that some of the menu items have little markings beside them or that they seem to be grayed out. Each one of these little symbols has a different meaning.

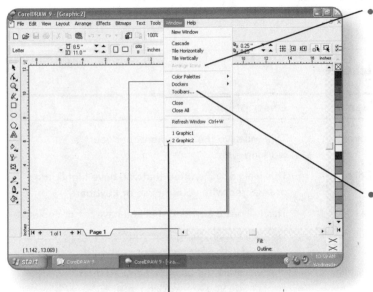

- **Gray or Dimmed Command.** This indicates that option is not currently available. There are a variety of reasons why a command may be dimmed; for example, under the Edit menu, the Copy command may be gray because it requires that something be selected first.

- **Three Dots.** This means that when you click on this menu item, a dialog box with more options related to that command will appear. You'll learn more about dialog boxes in the next section.

- **Check Mark.** A check mark means that the command is turned on or the option is selected. There are some commands that can either be on or off, for example, an automatic spell checker in a word processor. If you click on a menu option that already has a check mark beside it, it will then be turned off and the check mark will be gone.

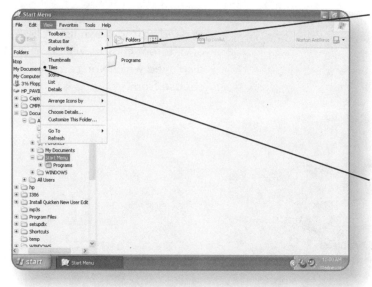

- **Triangle.** If there is a triangle beside a menu item, it means that there is a sub-menu that will appear when you click on this item. In other words, when you click on a command with a triangle beside it, another menu will appear with more choices.

- **Dot.** A dot beside a command in a menu indicates that this option is selected when only one option out of a few can be selected at a time. For example, in a word processor, you might have alignment options of center, left, or right justified. Only one of these can be selected at a time, so a dot would appear beside one of them.

Working with Dialog Boxes

When a program requires some information from you, it typically collects this information from a dialog box. Dialog boxes usually offer you choices in the form of a drop-down menu, check boxes, or empty fields. As different programs will ask for different information, not all dialog boxes will be alike. Some may require only one piece of information while others may have dozens of choices.

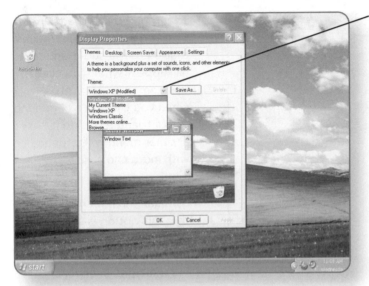

1. **Click** on the **down arrow** to expand a drop-down list. A list of different choices will be displayed which you can then choose from.

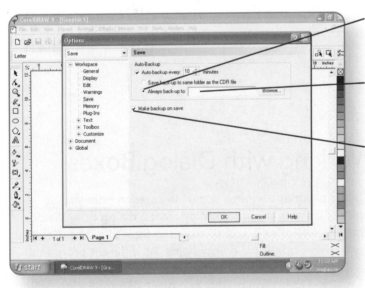

2. **Click** on a **circle radio button** to select between one of several options.

3. **Type** in a **field** to enter new data. These fields allow you to manually enter information.

4. **Click** in a **box** to select or deselect one or more options. In situations where you can select one or more than one option, a box appears. An x or a check mark in the box indicates that the option is selected.

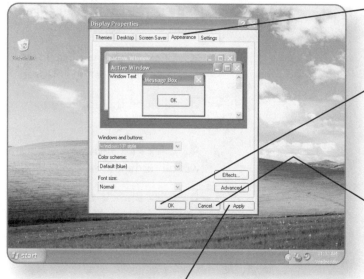

5. **Click** on the **desired tab** to toggle between different pages within a dialog box. Each page offers more options.

6a. **Click** the **OK** button. The changes that you have made will be applied and the dialog box will close.

OR

6b. **Click** the **Cancel** button. Any changes you have made will be ignored and the dialog box will close.

TIP

Occasionally, dialog boxes will have an Apply button. The Apply button lets you see the changes that you have made without committing to them. After you've clicked Apply, you can click OK to confirm the changes or click Cancel to disregard.

Ending Applications

Occasionally there may be times when a program becomes unstable and will no longer function properly. In older operating systems, this would require that you reboot your entire system. In Windows XP Media Center Edition, you can terminate just the program without having to reboot the computer.

1. **Press** the **Ctrl**, **Alt**, and **Delete** keys all at the same time. The Windows Task Manager dialog box will open.

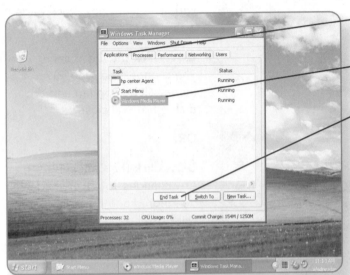

2. **Click** on the **Applications tab** if it is not already selected.

3. **Click** on the application that you would like to terminate.

4. **Click End Task**. The program will be terminated.

5. **Click** the **x** in the top right corner to close the Windows Task Manager.

Ending Your Session

When you are finished using your computer, you have a variety of options available to you. You can put your computer in a standby mode, you can log off, or you can shut down the computer completely.

Turning Off the Computer

This is the procedure for properly closing down your computer if you are completely finished with your session and want to turn the computer off.

1. Close any opened **applications** and make sure that you save anything that you were working on.

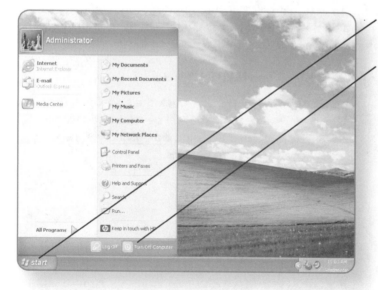

2. Click Start. The Start menu will appear.

3. Click Turn Off Computer. A dialog box of three options will now appear.

4. **Click Turn Off**. The computer will shut down.

Logging Off

Rather than turning off the computer entirely, you may wish to just log off and either log in as a different user or leave the computer available for someone else to log on.

1. **Click Start.** The Start menu will appear.

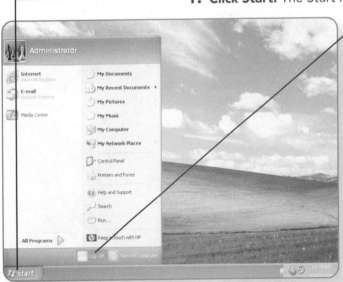

2. **Click** the **Log Off** button. You will be presented with a dialog box giving you two options.

3a. **Click** the **Switch User** button if you want to switch to another user that has access to this computer.

OR

3b. **Click** the **Log Off** button if you simply want to log off.

Restart

Occasions may arise where you will have to restart your computer. Typically this is the case after you've installed a new piece of software that requires a system reboot to load properly.

1. **Click Start.** The Start menu will appear.

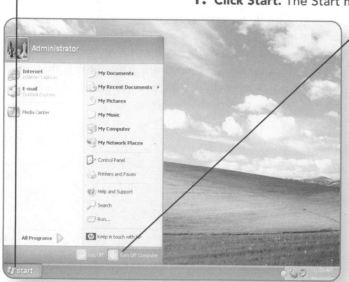

2. **Click Turn Off Computer.** A dialog box of three options will now appear.

3. **Click Restart**. The computer will shut down and then restart.

Hibernation

You're in the middle of working on a big report, you're searching the Web for information, you're typing in your word processor, and you're playing an MP3 file. Suddenly, you are called out of the office to a meeting. Rather than having to close and save all of the applications, you can put your computer into hibernation mode. Hibernation mode shuts down your computer while remembering everything that you were working on. When you restart your computer, it will restart in the same state that you left it.

1. Click Start. The Start menu will appear.

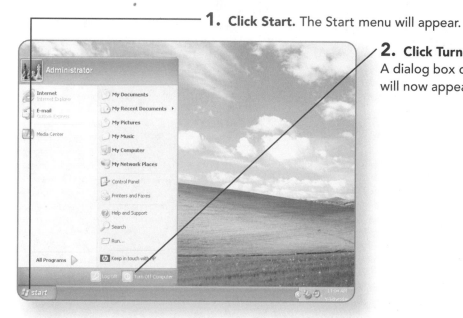

2. Click Turn Off Computer. A dialog box of three options will now appear.

3. Click Stand By. The computer will shut down. When you restart your computer, your desktop will return to its last state.

9

Customizing Windows XP

Your computer is really like no other appliance that you own. It can be completely customized to fit the individual personality of the person using it—now, what toaster oven can say that? Windows XP Media Center Edition allows you to customize just about every aspect of your computer experience. In this chapter, you'll learn how to:

- Customize the desktop
- Apply themes
- Adjust the Start menu
- Change sounds

Customizing the Desktop

Think of the desktop as your home base. Everything that you do on your computer starts from the desktop. The look, feel, and functionality of the desktop can be completely customized to fit your taste.

Changing the Background

The default picture that appears as the background image of the desktop in Windows XP Media Center Edition is of some rolling hills and a bright blue sky. You can change this and select from a variety of pre-installed backgrounds, or you can even upload one of your own digital photos.

Selecting a Pre-installed Image as a Desktop Background

Windows XP Media Center Edition comes with a variety of professional-quality photos that can be used as the background image for your desktop.

1. **Right-click** in any **blank area** of the desktop. A menu will appear.

2. **Click Properties**. This will open the Display Properties dialog box.

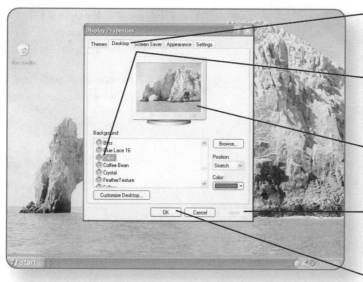

3. **Click** on the **Desktop tab**. Options for the desktop background will appear.

4. **Click** on a **Background**. You can scroll through the list and select from any of the pre-installed backgrounds. A preview of the background will appear in the picture of the monitor.

5. **Click Apply**. The picture will be inserted as the background image of your desktop.

6. **Click OK** if you are happy with the appearance of the new background; otherwise, select another background.

Using Your Own Image as a Desktop Background

You can use any digital image as the background for your desktop.

1. **Right-click** in any **blank area** of the desktop. A menu will appear.

2. **Click Properties**. This will open the Display Properties dialog box.

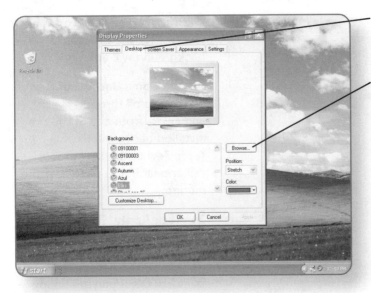

3. **Click** on the **Desktop tab**. Options for the desktop background will appear.

4. **Click Browse**. A dialog box will appear where you can select your image.

5. **Click** on the **image** you'd like to select.

NOTE

Windows XP Media Center Edition supports the following file types for background images: .bmp, .gif, .jpeg, .gpg, .png, .dib, .htm, and .html.

6. **Click Open**. The image will be loaded into the preview window.

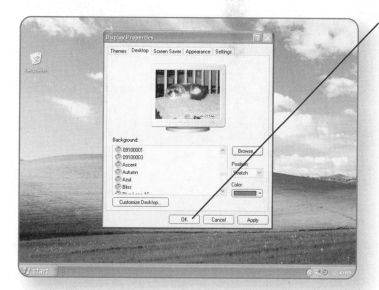

7. Click OK. The image will now be your desktop background.

Adding Icons to the Desktop

Icons represent a quick way to access programs, files, and folders that you would commonly use. Without having to sift through the Start menu, you can simply double-click on an icon and the program associated with that icon will launch.

Adding Common Icons

Depending on who manufactured your Windows XP Media Center computer, the number and types of icons that appear by default on your desktop will vary. If you have used a previous version of Windows in the past, you know that there are some common icons that give you access to frequently used programs and folders. Windows XP Media Center Edition offers a quick way to install these common icons.

1. **Right-click** in any **blank area** of the desktop. A menu will appear.

2. **Click Properties**. This will open the Display Properties dialog box.

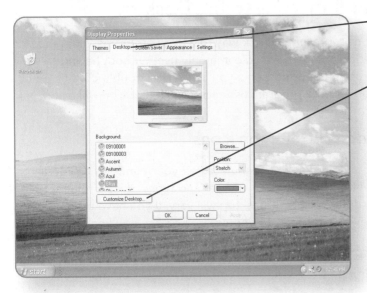

3. **Click** on the **Desktop tab**. Options for the desktop background will appear.

4. **Click Customize Desktop.** A dialog box will appear.

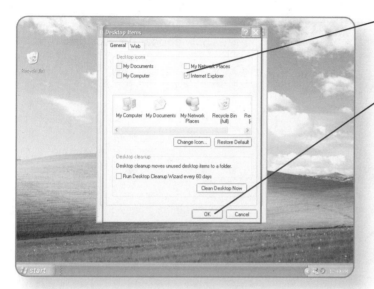

5. Click in the **box** beside the icons that you would like to add. A check mark will appear in the box, once it is selected.

6. Click OK. You will return to the previous dialog box.

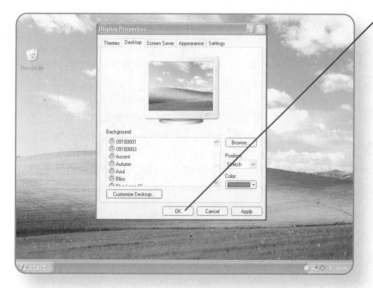

7. Click OK. The dialog box will close.

The icons that you selected will now appear on your desktop.

Adding Program Shortcuts

You can add a Shortcut icon of any program to your desktop so that you will have easy access to it. There are a variety of ways to create shortcuts on your desktop. Typically, you would have to know the location of the .exe file or .dll file that starts the program. With the following method, you can create a shortcut without having to browse through your computer's directory, looking for a specific file. In this example, we will create a shortcut for the game, Hearts, but you can repeat these steps for any program.

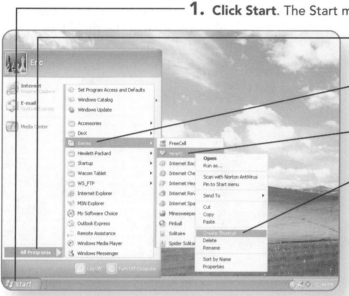

1. Click Start. The Start menu will appear.

2. Click All Programs. A list of programs will appear.

3. Click Games. A list of games will appear.

4. Right-click on **Hearts**. A menu will appear.

5. Click Create Shortcut. This will create another shortcut to Hearts in this location.

There will now be two instances of Hearts.

6. Click and **drag** the **second instance** of Hearts to the desktop.

7. Release the **mouse button**. The shortcut will be created.

NOTE

In this example, the number (2) appears after the Hearts icon. Later in the chapter, you will learn how to rename icons.

Removing a Desktop Icon

Because desktop icons are only shortcuts to programs, they can be deleted without affecting the program. The only exception to this is the Recycle Bin; it cannot be deleted.

1. Click and **drag** the **desktop icon** that you want to remove until it is over the Recycle Bin. The Recycle Bin will be highlighted, once the item is over it.

2. Release the **mouse button**. The icon will be sent to the Recycle Bin.

Renaming an Icon

You can easily change the name of an icon if you don't like the default name that it has been given.

1. **Right-click** on the **icon** that you would like to rename. A menu will appear.

2. **Click Rename**. You will now be able to type a new name for your icon.

3. **Type** a **name** for your icon. You can give it any name you like.

4. **Press Enter**. The icon will now have a new name.

Changing the Appearance of an Icon

The appearance of an icon is dependent on several factors, including what type of icon it is or what program is associated with it. Windows XP Media Center Edition allows you to change the appearance of your icons.

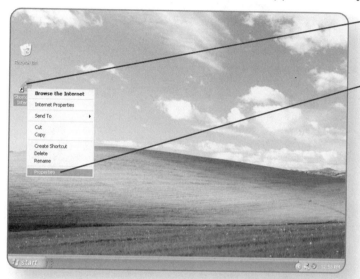

1. **Right-click** on the **icon** that you want to alter. A menu will appear.

2. **Click Properties**. This will open the Properties dialog box for this icon.

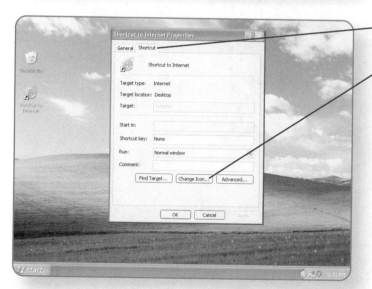

3. **Click** the **Shortcut tab** if it is not already selected.

4. **Click Change Icon**. You will now be able to choose a new icon.

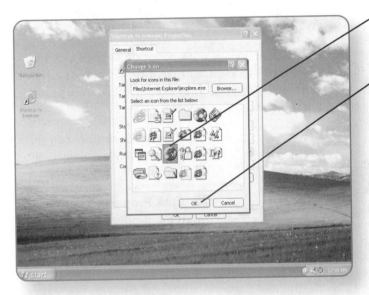

5. **Click** on the **desired icon**. It will be highlighted, once selected.

6. **Click OK**. You will be returned to the previous dialog box.

7. **Click OK**. The icon will now have the new look that you selected.

The Quick Launch Bar

The Quick Launch Bar is a bar that resides within the Taskbar. It allows you to add shortcuts of programs, just as you would on the desktop. The main difference is that the Quick Launch Bar is always visible, so you can always access any programs that are on the bar. Another difference is that shortcuts on the Quick Launch Bar can be launched with a single-click rather than a double-click.

Activating the Quick Launch Bar

When you first start using Windows XP Media Center Edition, by default, the Quick Launch Bar is not activated. You must first turn it on before it can be used. You can follow these same steps to remove the Quick Launch Bar.

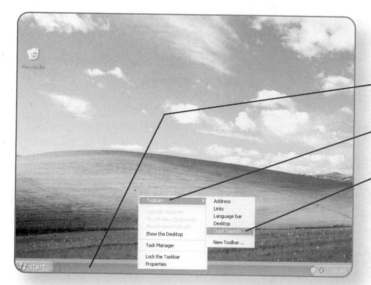

1. **Right-click** anywhere on the **Taskbar**. A menu will appear.

2. **Click Toolbars**. A list of different Toolbars will appear.

3. **Click Quick Launch**. The Quick Launch Bar will now be activated and will contain three shortcuts.

The Quick Launch Bar will appear beside the Start button with several icons activated.

Adding an Icon to the Quick Launch Bar

The procedure to creating a shortcut on the Quick Launch Bar is the same as creating one on the desktop, with only one added step. After the icon has been created on the desktop, it can be dragged onto the Quick Launch Bar.

1. Click Start. The Start menu will appear.

2. Click All Programs. A list of programs will appear.

3. Click Games. A list of games will appear.

4. Right-click on **Hearts**. A menu will appear.

5. Click Create Shortcut. This will create another shortcut to Hearts in this location.

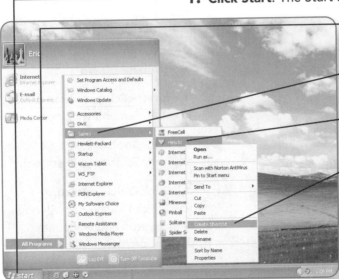

There will now be two instances of Hearts

6. **Click** and **drag** the **second instance** of Hearts to the desktop.

7. **Release** the **mouse button**. The shortcut will be created.

8. **Click** and **drag** the **shortcut** over the Quick Launch Bar. A little arrow will appear in the corner of the icon when it is over the bar.

9. **Release** the **mouse button**. The icon will be created on the Quick Launch Bar.

Removing an Icon from the Quick Launch Bar

The process of removing an icon from the Quick Launch Bar is simply a matter of clicking.

1. **Right-click** on the icon that you would like to delete. A menu will appear.

2. **Click Delete**. A dialog box will appear, confirming that you want to delete this icon.

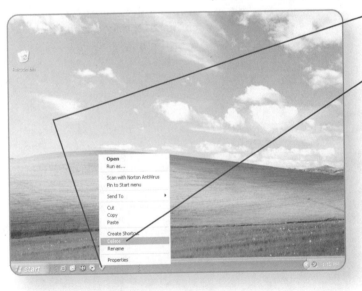

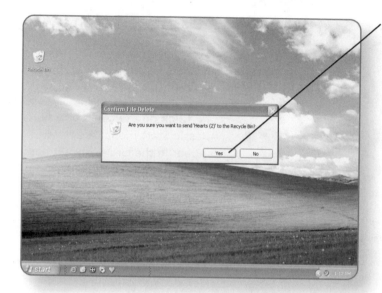

3. Click Yes. The icon will be removed from the Quick Launch Bar.

Customizing the Start Menu

The Start menu is always changing, adapting to the way in which you work with your computer. You'll find programs that you access often will appear directly in the Start menu. You can control many elements of the Start menu, including the size of the icons, the number of programs, and the look of the Start menu. Customizing the Start menu is done through the Properties dialog box.

1. Right-click on the **Start** button. A menu will appear.

2. Click Properties. The Properties dialog box will open and you can customize the Start menu.

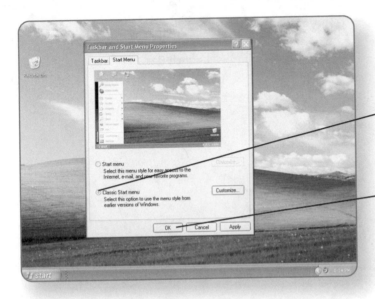

Classic Start Menu

If you have used earlier versions of Windows, you may prefer to use the Classic Start menu.

1. **Click** on the **circle** beside Classic Start menu. A dot will appear in the circle, once it has been selected.

2. **Click OK**. Your Start menu will now revert to its form from earlier versions of Windows.

Moving Programs on the Start Menu

Programs and shortcuts appear throughout the Start menu. Some programs fall into certain categories while others just appear on their own. You can change the location of programs simply by clicking and dragging.

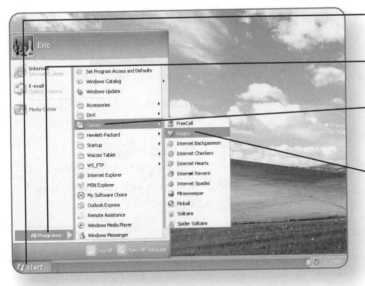

1. **Click Start**. The Start menu will appear.

2. **Click All Programs**. A list of all of your programs will appear.

3. **Click Games**. A list of programs in that category will appear.

4. **Position** your **mouse pointer** over the **program** that you'd like to move.

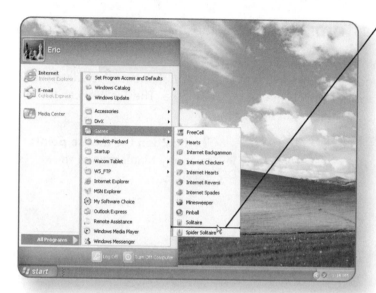

5. **Click** and **drag** the **program** to its new location. A black line will appear showing you where the program will be placed.

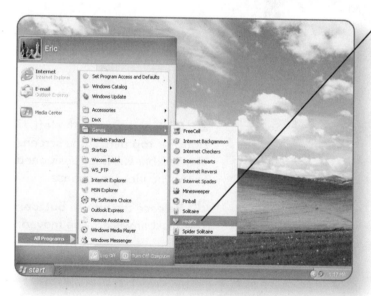

6. **Release** the **mouse button** and the program will be moved.

Customizing the Taskbar

The Taskbar, the long blue bar across the bottom of your page, contains some very important elements, including the Start button and the Notification area. The Taskbar can be moved, hidden, or locked.

1. **Position** the **mouse pointer** over any **blank area** of the Taskbar.

2. **Click** and **drag** to the **left, right,** or **top** part of the screen. The Taskbar will be repositioned to the location you choose.

3. **Release** the **mouse button.** The Taskbar will now be moved.

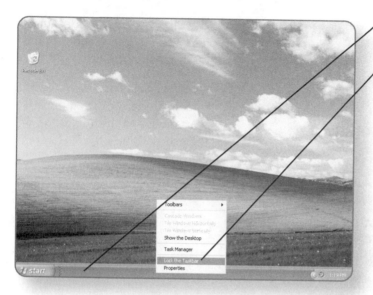

4. Right-click on the **Taskbar**. A menu will appear.

5. Click Lock the Taskbar. This will prevent it from being accidentally moved. You can unlock it by right-clicking and selecting Lock the Taskbar again.

Auto-Hiding the Taskbar

Some people prefer to have a completely uncluttered screen when they are working in programs. Because the Taskbar is so important to the operation of your computer, you wouldn't want to delete it. You can, however, put it in Auto-hide mode where it will remain hidden until you hover over the area with the mouse.

1. Right-click on the **Taskbar**. A menu will appear.

2. Click Properties. The Properties dialog box will open.

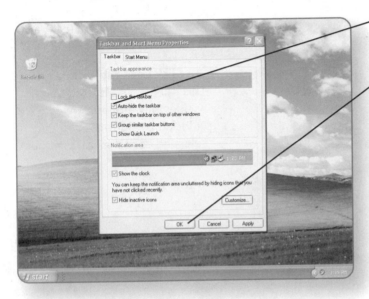

3. **Click** the **box** beside Auto-hide the taskbar. A check mark will appear in the box.

4. **Click OK**. The Taskbar will remain hidden until you move your mouse to the very edge of the screen where the Taskbar was located.

Screensavers

Originally, screensavers were designed to prevent computer monitors from phosphor burn-in. If the same image was being displayed in early monitors for a long time, the image would discolor the glass so that a faint overlay could always be seen, even if something else was being shown on the monitor. With modern monitors, screensavers aren't really necessary, but they provide an interesting way to personalize your computer.

1. **Right-click** in any **blank area** of the desktop. A menu will appear.

2. **Click Properties**. The Properties dialog box will open.

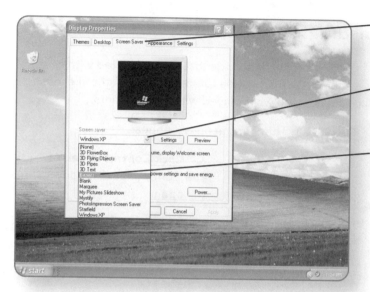

3. Click the **Screen Saver tab**. You will now be able to select from a range of screensavers.

4. Click the **down arrow** beside Screen saver. A list of screensavers will appear.

5. Click the **desired Screen saver**. A preview of the screensaver will appear in the picture of the monitor.

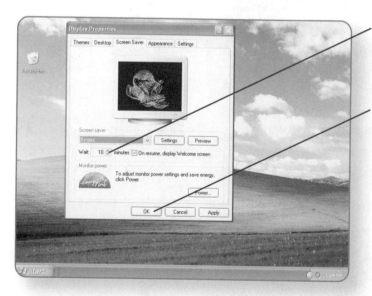

6. Click the **up or down arrows** to adjust the number of minutes to wait before the screensaver comes on.

7. Click OK. The settings will take effect.

Changing Sounds

There are a variety of sounds that are associated with certain tasks in Windows XP Media Center Edition. You can choose which sounds you want played with which events.

1. Click Start. The Start menu will appear.

2. Click Control Panel. The Control Panel window will open.

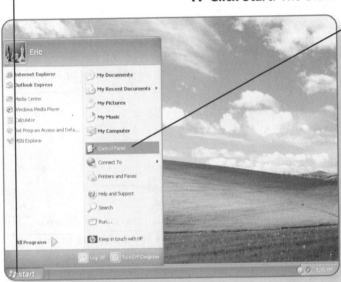

3. Click Sounds, Speech, and Audio Devices. You will now be prompted to pick a task.

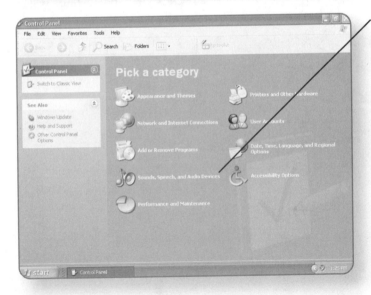

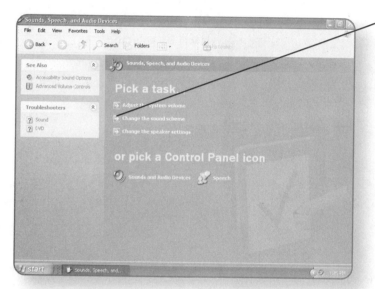

4. **Click Change the sound scheme**. A dialog box will open where you can set sounds for specific events.

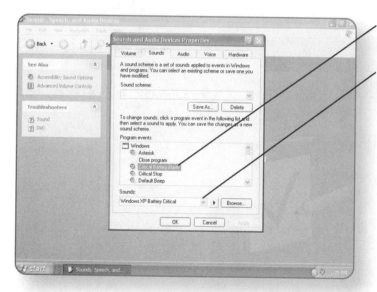

5. **Click** on an **event**. It will be highlighted.

6. **Click** on the **down arrow** beside Sounds. A list of different sounds will appear.

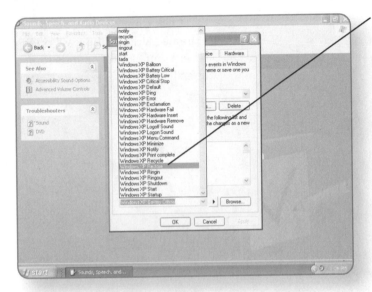

7. Click the **desired sound**. It will be selected.

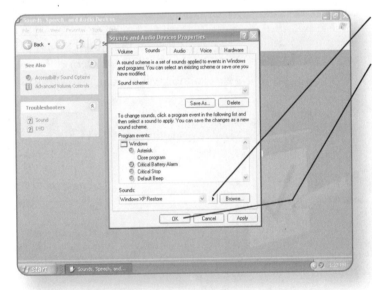

8. Click the **Play Sound** button to preview the sound.

9. Click OK. The changes will be saved.

10

Working with Programs

What would a computer be without programs to run on it? That isn't one of those if-a-tree-falls-in-a-forest type questions, it's really an easy one. Without programs to run on it, a computer is simply a piece of hardware with no function. There are literally hundreds of thousands of applications that you can run on your computer. Don't worry about having to run out and empty your wallet on new software, as Windows XP Media Center Edition comes with all of the software you need to get started. In this chapter, you'll learn how to:

- Use the Word Processor
- Use the Paint Program
- Use the Calculator

WordPad

WordPad is a word processing application that is installed with Windows XP Media Center Edition and that allows you to create and format documents and then save and output them.

Entering Text

Entering text into your document is as simple as just typing away.

1. Click Start. The Start menu will appear.

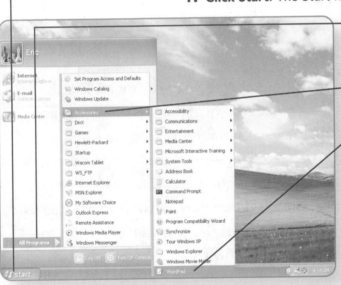

2. Click All Programs. A list of programs and program categories will appear.

3. Click Accessories. A list of accessory programs will appear.

4. Click WordPad. WordPad will be launched.

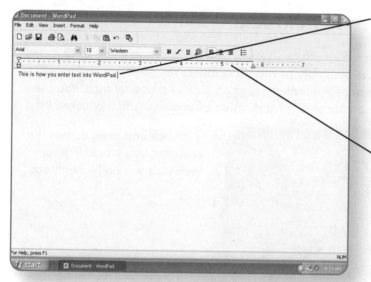

5. Type any **text**. As you type, the text will appear on the page. When you get to the end of the line, WordPad will automatically move to the next line.

NOTE

The Ruler indicates where you are relative to your page. WordPad will allow you to go beyond the margins of a normal page. Keep in mind that when you print your document, it may appear differently than it does on-screen as the text will be altered to fit the dimensions of the page.

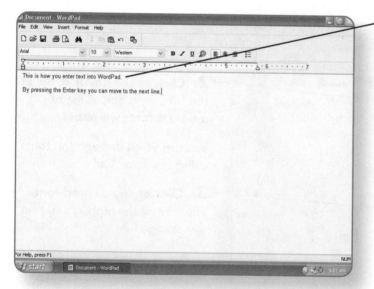

6. Press the **Enter** key to begin a new line. Every time you press Enter, you will start a new line.

Formatting Text

WordPad offers a variety of different formatting options that you can apply to your document. You have the ability to change the font style, color, size, and appearance. You can also change the justification of text and add a bulleted list.

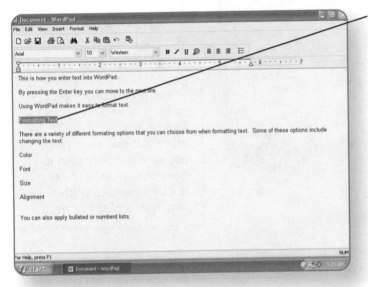

1. Click and drag across the **text** that you would like to format. It will be highlighted.

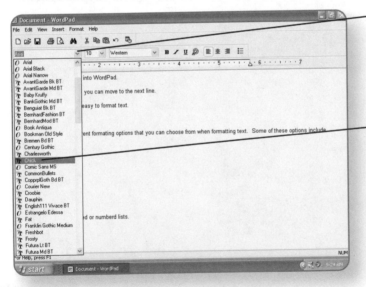

2. Click on the **down arrow** in the font style box. A list of different fonts will appear.

You can scroll through the fonts using the scroll bar.

3. Click on the **desired font**. The font of the highlighted text will change.

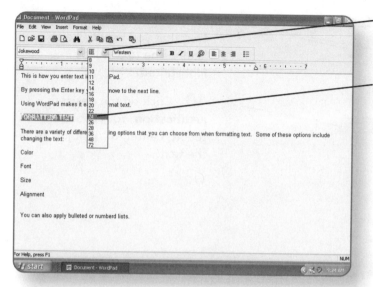

4. Click on the **down arrow** beside the font size box. A list of different font sizes will appear.

5. Click on the **desired font size**. The size of the highlighted text will change.

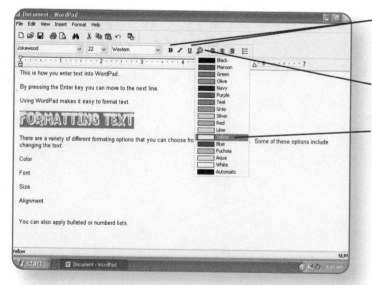

6. Click the **Bold**, **Italic**, and/or **Underline** button to apply that formatting to the selected text.

7. Click the **Color** button. A list of colors will appear.

8. Click on the **desired color**. The color of the highlighted text will change to the color you've selected.

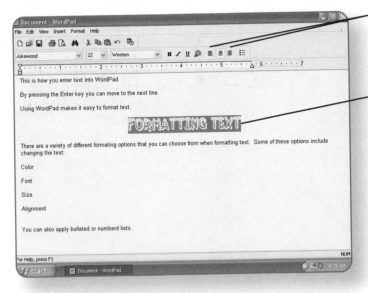

9. **Click** and **drag across** the **text** that you would like to justify. The text will be highlighted.

10. **Click** on the **desired justification**. Your choices are to left, center, or right justify the text.

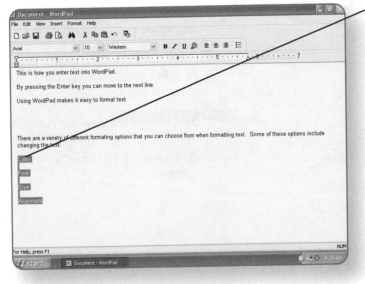

11. **Click** and **drag across** the **text** that you would like to create a bulleted list from. The text will be highlighted.

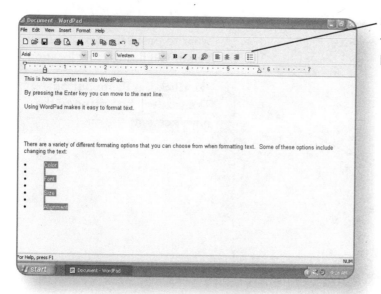

12. Click the **Bullets** button. The text you selected will now be formatted as a bulleted list.

Cutting, Copying, and Pasting Text

If you want to replicate parts of your document without having to retype them, you can use cut, copy, and paste. Cutting will remove text from a particular location to be used elsewhere, while copying will simply copy the text to the clipboard. Once an item has been placed on the clipboard, it can be reused indefinitely until something else is cut or copied.

1. Click and **drag** across the **text** that you want to cut.

2. Click the **Cut** button. The text will be removed from the document and placed on a virtual clipboard.

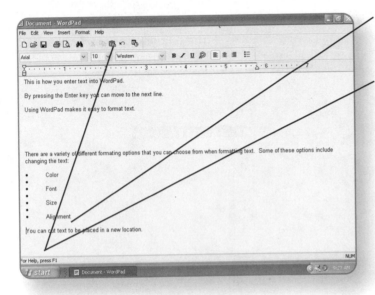

3. Click in the **area** where you want to paste the text. Your cursor will flash in that location.

4. Click the **Paste** button. The text will be pasted to the new location.

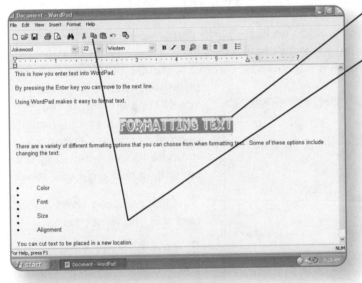

5. Click and **drag** across the **text** that you want to copy.

6. Click the **Copy** button. The text will remain in the document and a copy will be placed on a virtual clipboard.

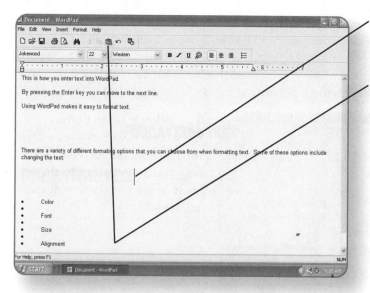

7. Click in the **area** where you want to paste the text. Your cursor will flash in that location.

8. Click the **Paste** button. The text will be pasted to the new location.

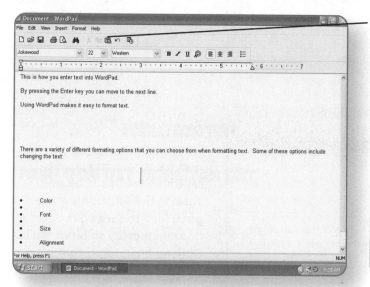

9. Click the **Paste** button **again**. Notice how even though it's been previously pasted, it remains on the virtual clipboard until something replaces it.

TIP

The keyboard shortcuts Ctrl+C and Ctrl+X can be used as the Copy and Cut commands. Ctrl+V can be used as the Paste command.

Undoing

If you have created some text or applied some formatting in error, rather than having to go back and delete it, you can use the Undo command. Every time you click the Undo button, you will be reverted back a step. Let's say for example you created text, changed its size, and then changed its color. If you click Undo once, the change of color will be removed. Click Undo again and the font size will be removed. Click Undo one more time, and you will be reverted back to the point before you created the text. You can use Undo to revert back to the point where the document was last saved.

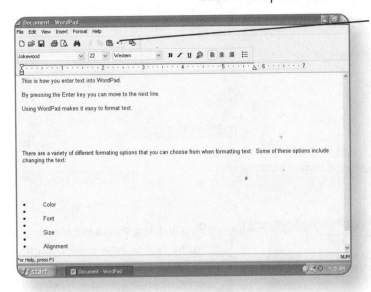

1. Click the **Undo** button. You will be reverted back a step. You can continue clicking Undo until you are reverted to the point where the document was last saved.

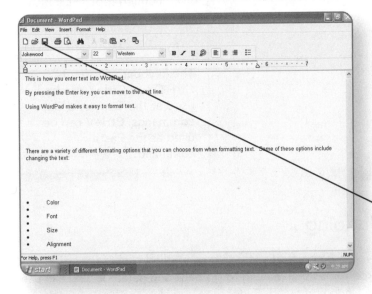

Saving

Once you've created a document, you may want to save it so that it can be used again in the future. It's also a good idea to save your document every so often, while working on it, to prevent accidental loss.

1. Click the **Save** button. The first time you click the Save button while working on a document, you will be prompted to give a name and location for the file. Every other time you click Save, the document will automatically be saved.

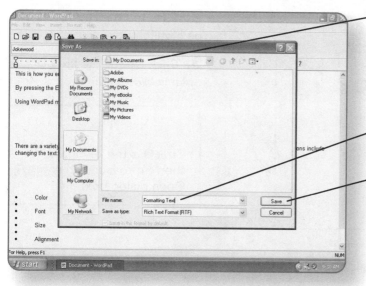

2. Click the **location** where you want to save the file. Windows XP Media Center Edition defaults to the My Documents folder, which is a good location to save your documents.

3. Type a **name** for the document you've created.

4. Click **Save**. The document will be saved to the location you've specified.

Opening a Document

You can open a document that has been created earlier or that someone has sent to you, using the Open command.

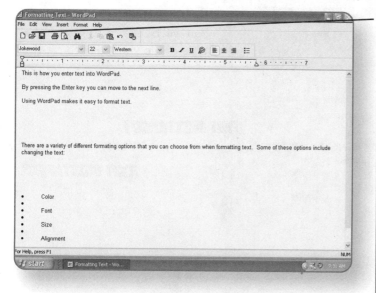

1. Click the **Open** button. A dialog box will appear where you can select the file that you'd like to open.

NOTE

WordPad supports files with the extension .txt, .wri, .doc, .rtf, and .htm. Depending on what program the document was originally created in, all of the original formatting for the document may not appear.

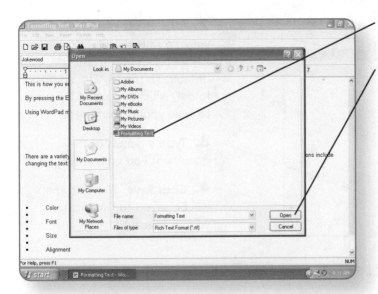

2. **Click** the **desired file**. It will be highlighted.

3. **Click Open**. The file will open in WordPad.

TIP

Ctrl+O is the keyboard shortcut to launch the Open dialog box.

Creating a New Document

To start a fresh new document, you can use the New command.

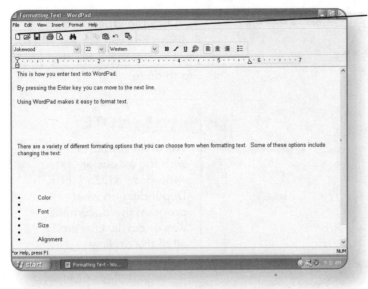

1. **Click** the **New** button. You will be asked to select what type of file you'd like to create.

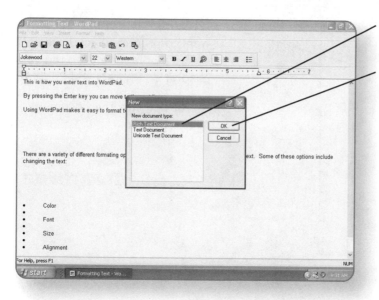

2. Click the **desired option**. It will be highlighted.

3. Click OK. A new document will be created.

Printing a Document

Most of the time, when you have completed a document, you'll probably want to print it out to distribute it.

1. Click File. The File menu will appear.

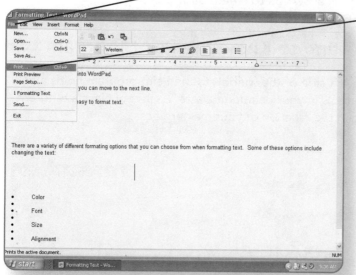

2. Click Print. The Print dialog box will appear.

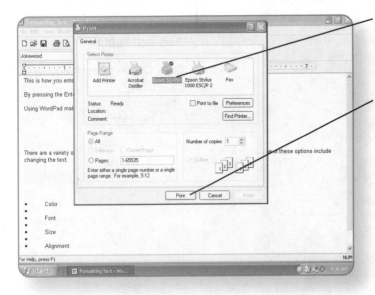

3. Click the **printer** that you want to print to. If you haven't set up a printer, refer to the chapter on Printers and Printing.

4. Click **Print**. The document will be printed.

Paint Program

Want to bring out your inner Picasso? The Paint program comes installed with a variety of painting and drawing tools that will allow you to create basic paintings.

Getting to Know the Paint Program

The left side of the window in the Paint program holds all of the tools in your painting palette. Each tool plays a different role in the creation of your masterpieces.

1. Click Start. The Start menu will appear.

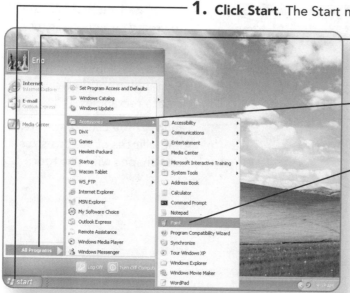

2. Click All Programs. A list of programs and categories will appear.

3. Click Accessories. The programs in the Accessories category will be displayed.

4. Click Paint. The Paint program will launch.

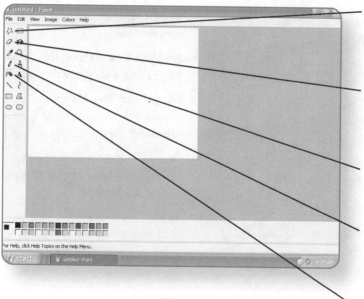

- **Free-Form Select.** With this tool, you can select objects on your page by drawing a free-form marquee around them.

- **Eraser/Color Eraser.** What's a pencil without an eraser? The Eraser tool allows you to remove parts of your diagram.

- **Pick Color.** This allows you to select a color and reapply it anywhere on your image.

- **Pencil.** The Pencil tool allows you to draw freehand lines that appear like a pencil drawing.

- **Airbrush.** Just like the T-shirts you get at the county fair, the Airbrush tool mimics real-life airbrushing.

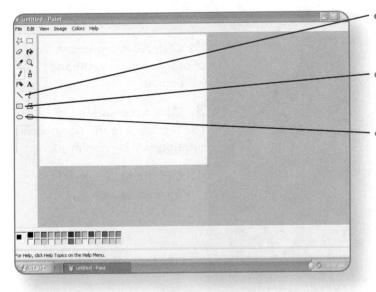

- **Line.** The Line tool allows you to create straight lines for your diagram.

- **Rectangle.** Guess what, the Rectangle tool allows you to create rectangles.

- **Ellipse.** You can create circles and ellipses of various sizes and shapes with this tool.

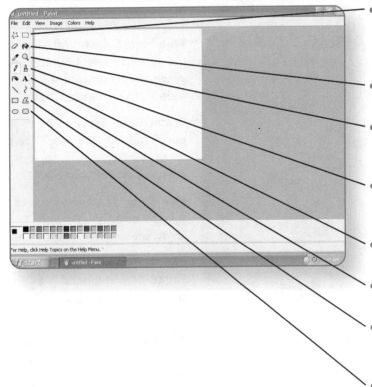

- **Select.** This tool allows you to select objects by drawing a rectangular marquee around them.

- **Fill With Color.** Using this tool, you can fill a shape with a color.

- **Magnifier.** The Magnifier allows you to zoom into different areas of your image.

- **Brush.** This tool acts as your paintbrush and can be altered in size and shape.

- **Text.** This tool allows you to add text to your images.

- **Curve.** To create curved lines, click this tool.

- **Polygon.** The Polygon tool allows you to create shapes with multiple sides.

- **Rounded Rectangle.** To create a rectangle with rounded edges, use this tool.

Creating Basic Shapes

There are three basic Shapes tools that can be used to create shapes by simply clicking and dragging on the page. You can adjust the size and shape by controlling how long you drag the mouse.

1. **Click** the **Ellipse** tool. The button will appear depressed.

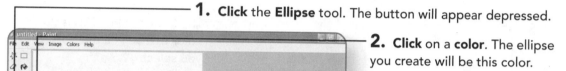
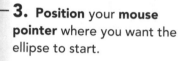

2. **Click** on a **color**. The ellipse you create will be this color.

3. **Position** your **mouse pointer** where you want the ellipse to start.

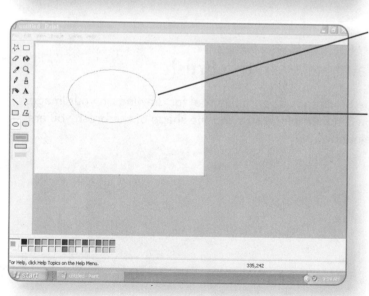

4. **Click** and **drag** in a **diagonal** motion. As you drag, a preview of what your ellipse will look like will appear.

5. **Release** the **mouse button**. The shape will be created.

Filling Shapes with Color

The Fill With Color tool allows you to fill closed areas with the color of your choice.

1. **Click** the **Fill With Color** tool. The button will appear depressed.

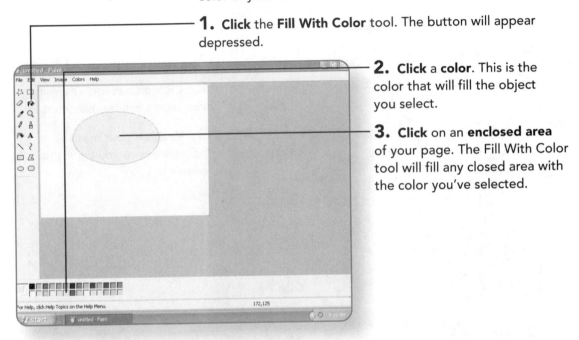

2. **Click** a **color**. This is the color that will fill the object you select.

3. **Click** on an **enclosed area** of your page. The Fill With Color tool will fill any closed area with the color you've selected.

Painting with the Brush

The Brush tool is your main tool for drawing on your image. You can control the size and the shape of the brush you are painting with.

1. **Click** the **Brush** tool. The button will appear depressed.

2. **Click** on the **desired shape and size** of the brush.

3. **Click** a **color**. This will be the color of your paint.

4. **Position** your **mouse pointer** where you'd like to start painting.

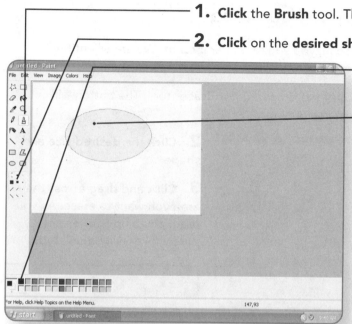

5. **Click** and **drag** on the **page**. As you drag, paint will be applied to the page.

Erasing Your Image

OK, so maybe you're no Rembrandt. We are all entitled to make mistakes while we are drawing our image.

1. Click the **Eraser/Color Eraser** tool. The button will appear depressed.

2. Click the **desired size and shape**.

3. Click and **drag** across the **area** you want to erase. As you drag, anything your eraser passes over will be deleted.

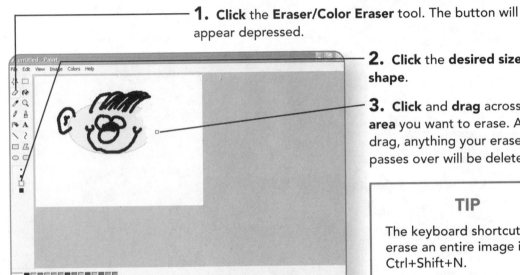

TIP

The keyboard shortcut to erase an entire image is Ctrl+Shift+N.

The Calculator

Why can you never seem to find a calculator when you need one? Well, that'll no longer be the case, because when you're running Windows XP Media Center Edition, there is always a calculator on hand. The calculator can be used with either the numeric keypad or your keyboard. The calculator has both a standard and scientific mode.

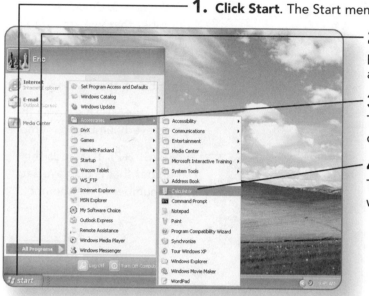

1. **Click Start**. The Start menu will appear.

2. **Click All Programs**. A list of programs and categories will appear.

3. **Click Accessories.** The programs in the Accessories category will be displayed.

4. **Click Calculator.** The Calculator program will launch.

Getting to Know the Calculator

The numbers and normal operations on the standard calculator make sense, but what do all those other numbers do?

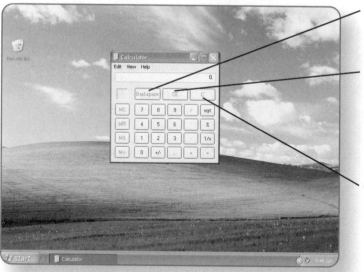

• **Backspace.** Pressing this will move your cursor back one space.

• **CE** (Del). Clears the displayed number. If you erroneously enter a number, click this button to remove the number without having to clear your entire calculation.

• **C** (Esc). Clears everything from the calculation area. Press this button when you want to start a fresh calculation.

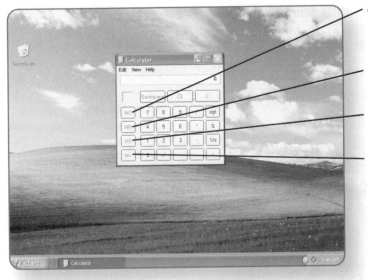

- **MC** (Ctrl+L). Clears any number that you stored in memory.

- **MR** (Ctrl+R). Recalls the number in the memory.

- **MS** (Ctrl+M). This stores the displayed number in memory.

- **M+** (Ctrl+P). This adds the number that is displayed to the number in the memory.

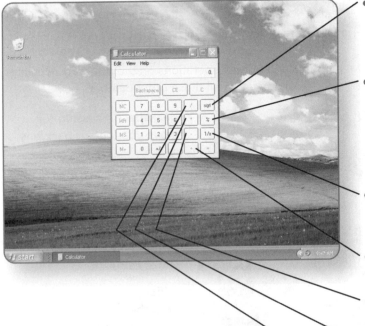

- **Sqrt** (@). Clicking this button will calculate the square root of any number that you have displayed.

- **%** (%). If you want to display the results of a division as a percentage, click this button. For example, if you wanted to know what 25% of 100 is, you would click 100 * 25 %.

- **1/x** (R). This will calculate the reciprocal of the number entered.

- **+** (+). This is the addition operator.

- **-** (-). This is the subtract operator.

- ***** (*). This is the multiply operator.

- **/** (/). This is the divide operator.

Using the Calculator

This electronic calculator works the same way a typical calculator works. You simply type or click the digits and operators.

1. **Click** a **number**. The number will be displayed.

2. **Click** on the **desired operator**.

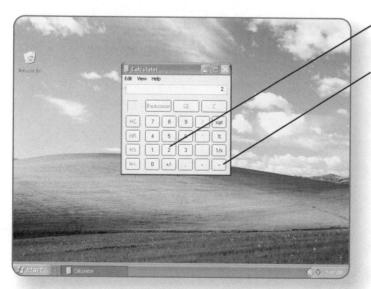

3. **Click another digit**. It will be displayed.

4. **Click** the **equals** button. The result will be displayed in the window.

Using the Calculator Data

Once you've completed your calculations, you may want to use the results in other programs. To do that, you can make use of the clipboard feature.

1. **Click Edit**. The Edit menu will appear.

2. **Click Copy**. The number displayed will be copied to the clipboard.

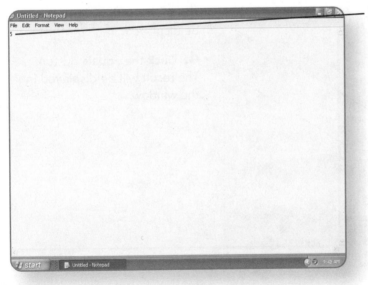

3. **Click Ctrl+V** in almost any other program to paste the data.

11

File Management

Imagine that instead of using a filing cabinet, every time you created a file or folder, you simply threw it on the floor. After a while, the mountain of files would be so big that finding and using a specific file or folder would be impossible. The same holds true for files and folders that you create on your computer. If you didn't have a proper file management system, accessing things you've created on your computer would be a daunting task. The good news is that Windows XP Media Center Edition comes with amazing file management capabilities. In this chapter, you'll learn how to:

- Navigate through the files and folders on your computer
- Create, name, and delete files and folders
- Copy, move, and rename files and folders
- Customize the appearance of a file or folder

Navigating Through Your Computer

Windows XP Media Center Edition comes with a variety of ways to view and manage the many files and folders on your computer. The tool that is designed specifically for managing your files is called My Computer. My Computer is a window that will give you a visual image of the contents of your computer.

Launching My Computer

My Computer is easily accessed from the Start menu of your computer.

1. Click the **Start** button. The Start menu will appear.

2. Click My Computer. The My Computer window will appear.

Navigating My Computer

The files and folders on your computer are set up in a hierarchical structure. At the top of the hierarchy, you'll find your storage device, whether it is a hard disk, a CD, or a floppy disk. Within that storage device, you'll find either files or folders, or both. Any folders can then contain subfolders. The My Computer window allows you to view the contents on your machine at a glance.

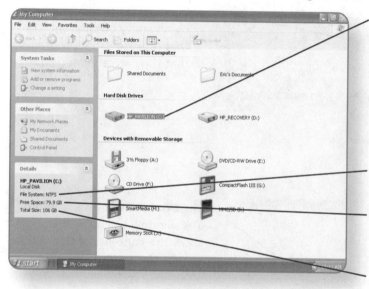

1. Click on the **hard drive** or the **storage device** whose contents you want to view. The object will be highlighted. Once selected, the Details section of the window will change to give you information on the drive, file, or folder you've selected.

- **File System.** This indicates how the disk was formatted.

- **Free Space.** The amount of unused space you have on that drive.

- **Total Size.** The total amount of both used and unused space on that drive.

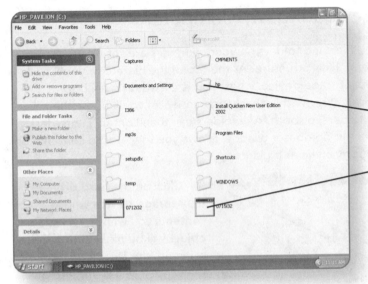

2. **Double-click** on the **hard drive** or the **storage device** whose contents you want to view. The window will change to show you the contents of that device.

- **Folders.** An icon that looks like a manila folder represents folders.

- **Files.** Files are represented by a variety of different icons that represent the programs that they are affiliated with.

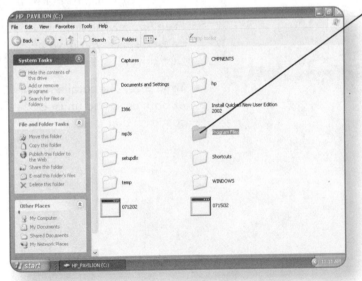

3. **Double-click** on any **folder**. The window will now change to show the contents of that folder.

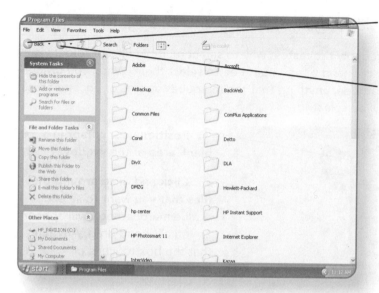

4. Click Back. This will take you to the window that you were previously viewing.

5. Click the **Forward** button. This will return you to the window you were viewing before you hit the Back button.

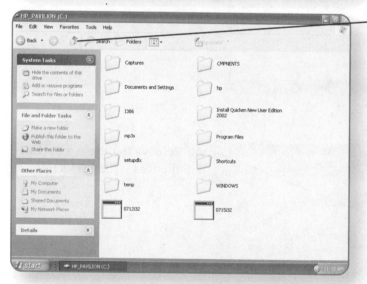

6. Click the **Up** button. This will take you up a level in the hierarchy.

Managing Files

The My Computer window makes managing files and folders on your computer easy by offering the ability to create, move, delete, and rename a file at the click of a mouse button. It even gives you the ability to publish a file to the Web or e-mail it.

Selecting Multiple Files

If you want to perform a file management task on a single file, the process is quite simple. You just have to click on the file and then perform the desired task. To save some time, you may want to perform a task like moving, copying, or deleting on multiple files all at once. To do this, Windows XP Media Center Edition provides you with a variety of methods for selecting multiple files and folders.

Selecting by Clicking and Dragging

Probably the fastest way to select multiple files or folders is to click and drag a marquee to select them. When you drag a marquee, anything that the marquee touches or encompasses will be selected.

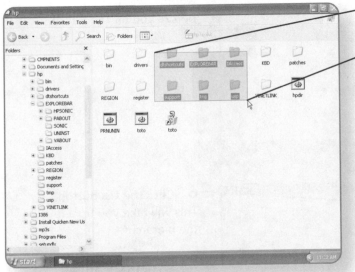

1. **Position** your **cursor** in a **blank area** of the window.

2. **Click** and **drag around** the **files** that you want to select. A blue marquee box will appear as you click and drag. Anything that the box touches or encompasses will be selected.

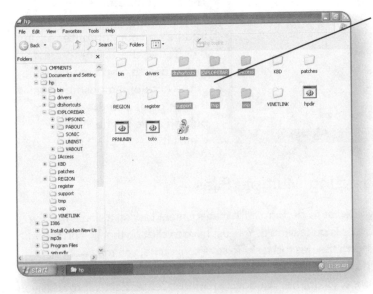

3. **Release** the **mouse button** and the files will be selected.

Selecting with the Shift Key

Another way to select multiple files is by using the Shift key along with your mouse. The Shift key allows you to select multiple adjacent files.

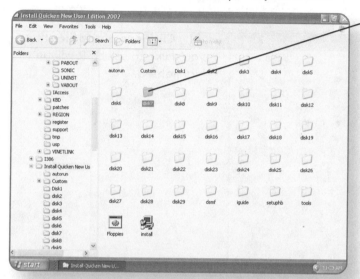

1. **Click one** of the **files** that you'd like to select. It will be highlighted.

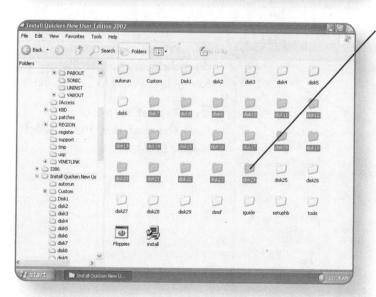

2. **Press Shift** and at the same time **click** on **another file** that you'd like to select. All the files in between the first file selected and the one you just clicked will be selected.

Selecting with the Ctrl Key

One of the limitations of using both the click and drag and the Shift key method of selecting is that all of the files that you want to select must be grouped together. In order to select files that are not adjacent, you can use the Ctrl key method.

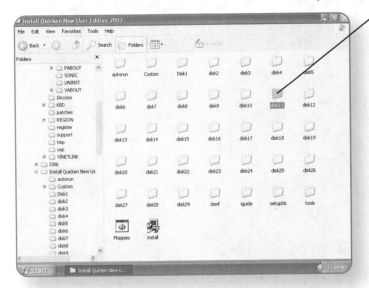

1. **Click one** of the **files** that you'd like to select. It will be highlighted.

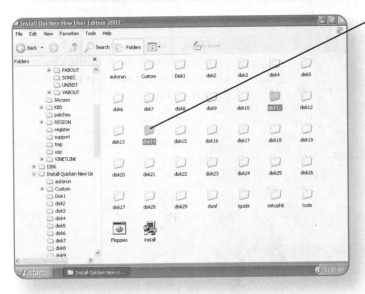

2. **Press Ctrl** and at the same time **click** on **another file** or folder that you'd like to select.

3. **Repeat Step 2** until you have selected all of the desired files or folders.

Deselecting Files

If you've made a mistake while selecting files or folders, you can choose to deselect an individual file or the entire selection.

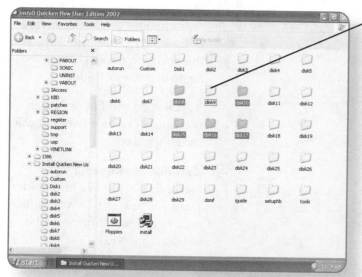

1. Press Ctrl and **click** on a **file** you'd like to deselect. That individual file or folder will be removed but the rest of the selection will remain.

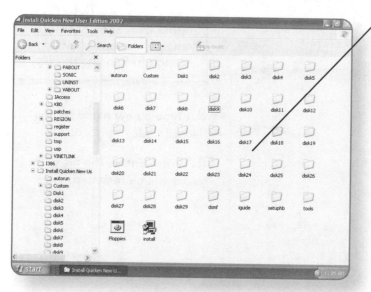

2. Click once **anywhere** in a **blank area** of the window. Any selected files or folders will be deselected.

Renaming a File

I can't tell you how many Document1, Document2, and Document3 files there are on my computer. Without giving a file a descriptive name, file management can become very difficult. My Computer gives you the ability to easily change the name of a file or folder.

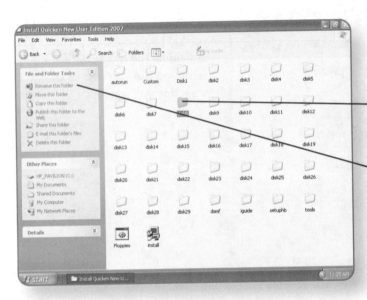

1. Click on the **file** or **folder** that you'd like to rename. It will be highlighted.

2. Click the **Rename this folder** link in the File and Folder Tasks window. A box will appear around the folder name and it will be highlighted.

NOTE

If you have selected a file rather than a folder to rename, the option will change to Rename this file.

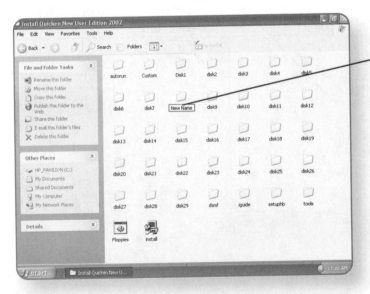

3. Type a **new name** for the file or folder.

4. Press Enter. The file or folder will be renamed.

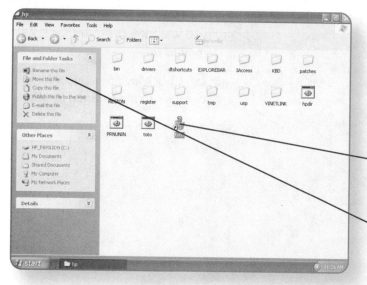

Moving a File or Folder

If you want to change where a certain file or folder is located on your computer, the My Computer window makes it a breeze.

1. Click the **file** or **folder** that you'd like to move. It will be highlighted.

2. Click the **Move this file** link in the File and Folder Tasks area of the window. A Move Items dialog box will appear where you can select where on the computer you'd like to move the file or folder.

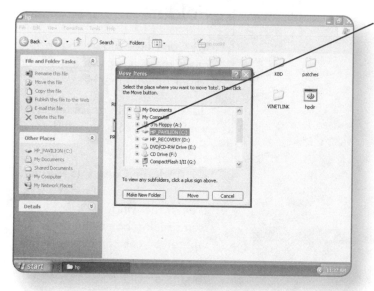

3. Click on the + beside the storage device where you want to move the file. If you just want to move it to the storage device and not within a specific folder, simply click on the storage device and skip to Step 5.

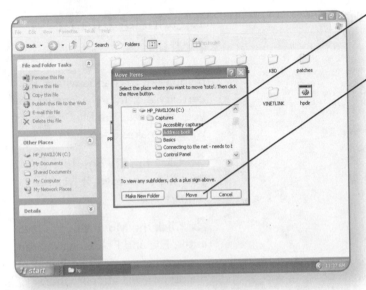

4. **Click** on the **folder** where you want the file or folder moved to.

5. **Click Move** to move the file or folder to the selected location.

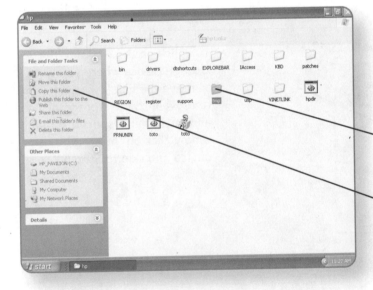

Copying a File or Folder

My Computer allows you to easily make a copy of any file or folder on your machine.

1. **Click** the **file** or **folder** that you'd like to copy. It will be highlighted.

2. **Click** the **Copy this folder** link in the File and Folder Tasks area of the window. A Copy Items dialog box will appear where you can select where on the computer you'd like to copy the file or folder.

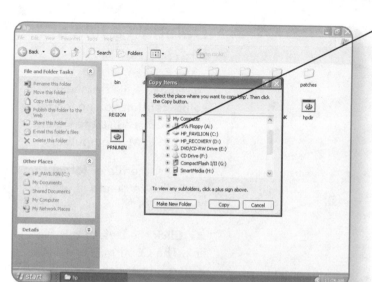

3. Click on the + beside the storage device where you want to copy the file. If you just want to copy it to the storage device and not within a specific folder, simply click on the storage device and skip to Step 5.

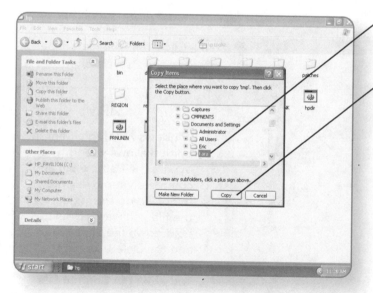

4. Click on the **folder** where you want the file or folder copied to.

5. Click Copy to copy the file or folder to the selected location.

Deleting a File or Folder

To remove a file from your computer that you no longer need, you can use the Delete function in My Computer.

1. Click the **file** or **folder** that you'd like to delete. It will be highlighted.

2. Click the **Delete this file** link. The Confirm File Delete dialog box will appear, asking if you are sure you want to send this to the Recycle Bin.

3. Click Yes. The file will be sent to the Recycle Bin.

TIP

Windows XP Media Center Edition allows you to bypass the Recycle Bin and completely remove a file or folder. To do this, select the file you want to delete, hold down the Shift key and the Delete key at the same time. You then click Yes when the Confirm File Delete dialog box appears.

Creating a Folder

To help you organize your files into logical groups, you can create your own folders. You can create a main folder on your hard drive or you can create a folder within any other folder.

1. Navigate to the **location** where you want to create your new folder.

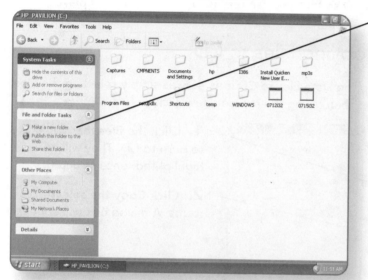

2. Click Make a new folder. A folder will be created in that location and you will be prompted to give it a name.

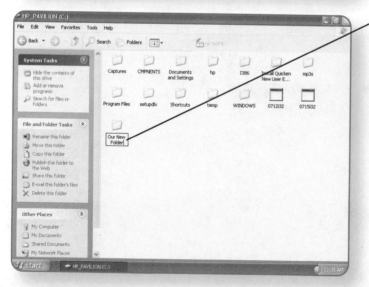

3. Type a **name** for your folder. You can choose any name for your folder.

4. Press Enter. The new folder will be created with the name you have given it.

Copying to a CD

Because every Windows XP Media Center Edition PC comes with a built-in CD Writer, you can burn files to be stored on compact disc. There are basically two different files that you can burn: data files or music files. Windows XP Media Center Edition allows you to convert digital music files to audio files on CD so that you can play your songs in any CD player.

Copying Files to CD

Storing Data files to CD is as easy as simply selecting the files and then giving the mouse a few clicks.

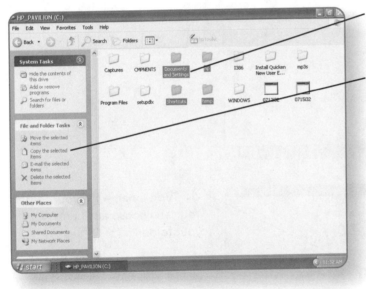

1. Click the **files** that you'd like to burn to CD. They will be highlighted, once selected.

2. Click Copy the selected items. A dialog box will appear.

3. **Insert** a **blank CD** in the CD Writer drive.

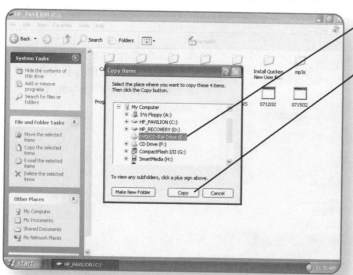

4. **Click** on the **drive** that represents the CD Writer.

5. **Click Copy.** The files will be copied to the CD.

Creating an Audio CD

You can create an audio CD that can be played in any CD player from your digital music files.

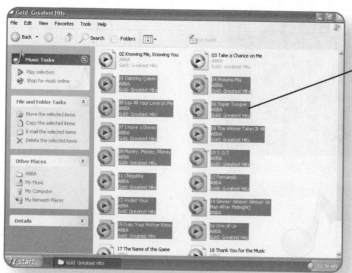

1. **Insert** a **blank CD** into the CD Writer.

2. **Click** the **audio files** that you'd like to include on your CD. They will be highlighted, once selected. You can use the Ctrl or Shift key to select multiple files.

3. **Right-click** on **any** of the **selected files**. A menu will appear.

4. **Click Copy to Audio CD.** Windows Media Player will launch with the files you've selected laid out.

5. **Click Copy Music.** The disc will be created.

12

Searching Your Computer

Remember the last time you lost your keys? If you're like most people, you were scrambling all over the house, using choice words, and repeatedly checking places you just looked. Wouldn't it be nice if you could press a button and you'd be told the exact location of those !@$!* keys? Even with a good file management system, it's still possible to lose track of where you've stored a file on your computer. The Search function built into Windows XP Media Center Edition allows you to find just about anything on your computer. In this chapter, you'll learn how to:

- Search for files and folders
- Work with Search results
- Search for multimedia files
- Search for people

Searching for Files and Folders

The Search tool within Windows XP Media Center Edition is an exceptional tool for digging through the mountains of files and folders on a computer to find the one you are looking for.

1. Click the **Start** button. The Start menu will appear.

2. Click Search. The Search window will now open.

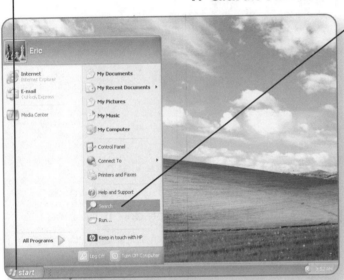

3. Click All files and folders. You will now be able to enter the criteria for your search.

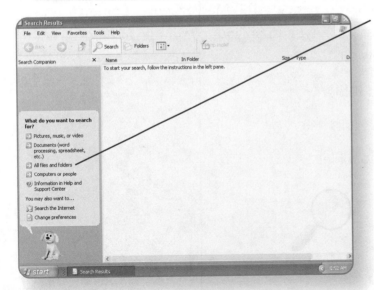

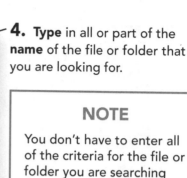

4. Type in all or part of the **name** of the file or folder that you are looking for.

NOTE

You don't have to enter all of the criteria for the file or folder you are searching for. Simply enter as much information as you have to help expedite the search. Don't worry about filling in every piece of information; date, name, size, and so on—just provide as much information as you have.

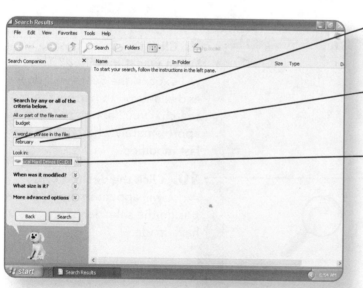

5. Press the **Tab** key. The cursor will now be in the next field box.

6. Type in a **word or phrase** that the file contains, if you happen to know.

7. Click the **down arrow** beside the **Look in** box. This is the place you specify where on the computer you'd like to search.

TIP

If you select the My Computer option, the search will look in every drive and folder on your computer.

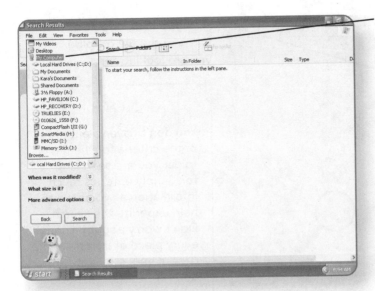

8. **Click** the **desired location** that you would like to search.

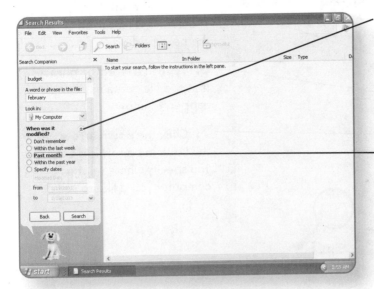

9. **Click** the **arrow** beside **When was it modified?** This will expand the Search window and allow you to narrow the search if you happen to know approximately when the file was last modified.

10. **Click** the **desired option**. A dot will appear in the circle beside the selection you have made.

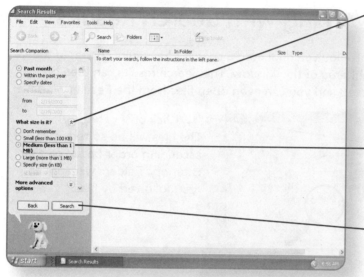

11. **Click** the **arrow** beside **What size is it?** More search options will appear that will allow you to narrow the search if you happen to know the approximate size of the file you're searching for.

12. **Click** the **desired option**. A dot will appear in the circle beside the selection you have made.

13. **Click** the **Search** button. The Search will be conducted and the result will appear on the right side of the window.

NOTE

Depending on the type of your computer, the number of files, and the amount of Search criteria provided, the length of time to conduct a search will vary.

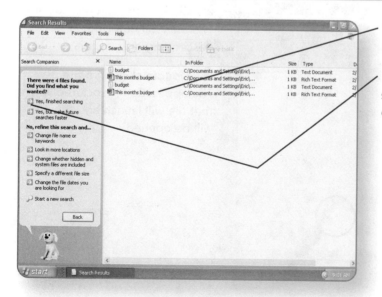

14. **Double-click** on a **result** to open that file or folder.

15. **Click Yes, finished searching** and the search will be completed.

Working with Search Results

Once you've conducted a search, the results appear in the right area of the window. The Search results can then be sorted and you can even open files from the Results window.

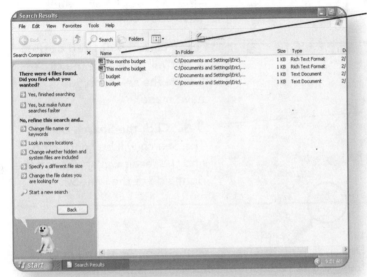

1. Click on a **category**.
The files will be sorted in ascending order based on that category. Folders will appear first, followed by files.

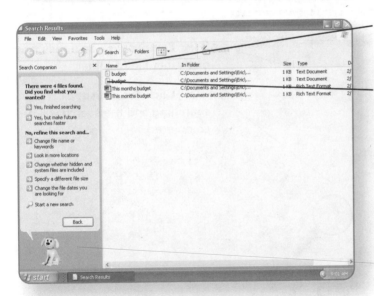

2. Click on the **same category**.
The files will now appear in descending order.

3. Double-click on a **file**.
The application associated with that file will launch and the file will be opened.

Searching for Multimedia

There's a good chance that you'll have a variety of multimedia files on your computer—after all, Windows XP Media Center Edition is specifically designed with video, music, and pictures in mind. A Search option specifically designed to help you find your multimedia files is built into the Operating System.

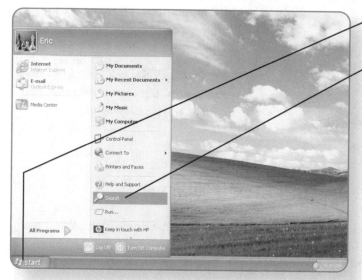

1. **Click** the **Start** button. The Start menu will appear.

2. **Click Search**. This will open the Search Results window.

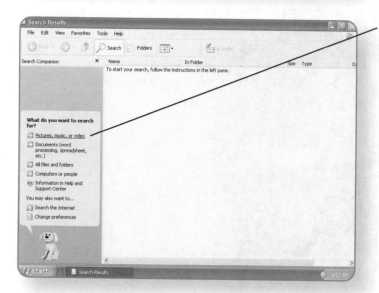

3. **Click Pictures, music, or video**. You will now be able to select the Search criteria.

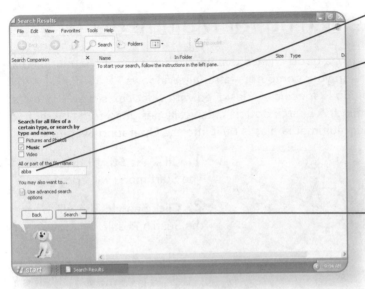

4. **Click** the desired **multimedia file type** you are looking for.

5. **Type** in all or some of the **file name**. This step is optional. If you are looking for all of a particular media type—for example, all of the music on your computer—simply check the Music option and click Search without entering a file name.

6. **Click Search**. All of the files that match the criteria that you set will be displayed.

Searching for People

If you've set up the Address Book that comes with Windows XP Media Center Edition, you can search for people using the Search Tool. For more information on creating an address book, see the Chapter entitled The Address Book.

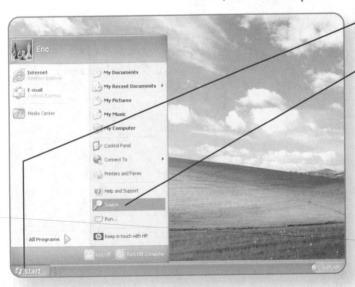

1. **Click** the **Start** button. The Start menu will appear.

2. **Click Search**. This will open the Search Results window.

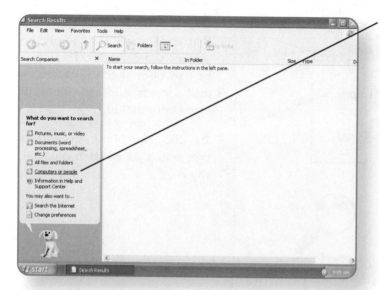

3. Click Computers or people. You will now need to choose whether you are looking for a computer on the network or a person in your address book.

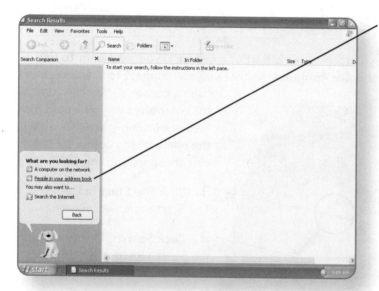

4. Click People in your address book. The window will change so you can search your address book.

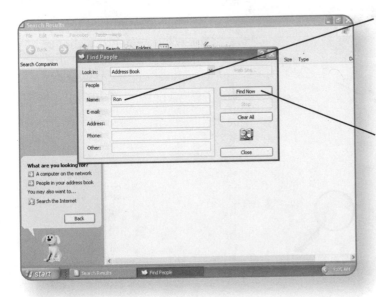

5. Type the **Search criteria** that you know about the person you are searching for. This can be part of or all of their name, e-mail address, address, phone, or other information.

6. Click **Find Now**. Any entries that match your search will be shown.

Searching for Computers

If your computer is part of a network, you may want to find a particular computer so that you can connect to it and view or use its contents. You can search for computers as you would for files—you simply have to know the name of the computer that you are searching for.

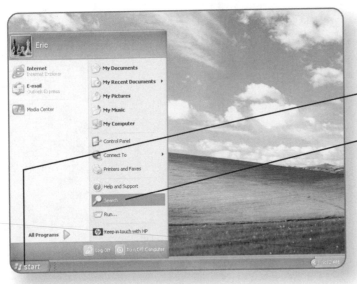

1. Click the **Start** button. The Start menu will appear.

2. Click **Search**. This will open the Search Results window.

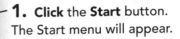

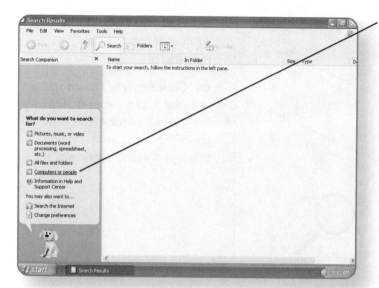

3. Click Computers or people. You will now need to choose whether you are looking for a computer on the network or a person in your address book.

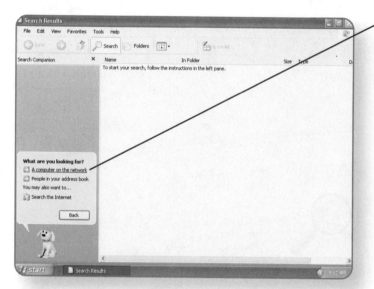

4. Click A computer on the network. You will now be prompted to enter the name of the computer you are looking for.

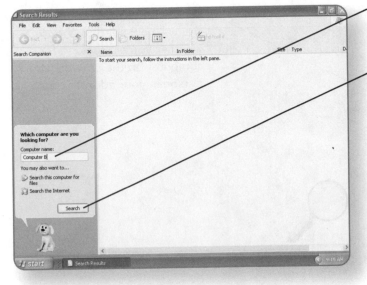

5. **Type** the **name** of the computer that you are looking for.

6. **Click Search**. The computer will search the network, looking for the computer name you specified. The results will be displayed in the window.

13

The Recycle Bin

No heavy lifting, no straining your back, no walking to the curb, and no having to deal with the elements. Taking out the Recycle Bin within Windows XP Media Center Edition is as easy as a few clicks of the mouse button. When you decide that you no longer need a file, folder, or icon, it is not permanently removed from your computer; rather, it is first sent to the Recycle Bin. The Recycle Bin acts as a safety net so that you don't inadvertently delete any files from your computer. In this chapter, you'll learn how to:

- Send files to the Recycle Bin
- View the contents of the Recycle Bin
- Restore files from the Recycle Bin
- Change the capacity of the Recycle Bin

Sending Files to the Recycle Bin

There are a variety of ways that you can place unwanted files or folders into the Recycle Bin. The two easiest methods are by either clicking and dragging or using the keyboard.

Sending Files to the Recycle Bin with the Keyboard

One of the easiest ways to move a file to the Recycle Bin is to use the Delete key on your keyboard.

1. Position your **mouse pointer** over the **file, folder, or icon** that you want to send to the Recycle Bin.

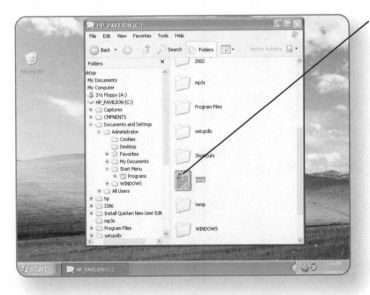

2. Click once to select it. It will be highlighted, once selected.

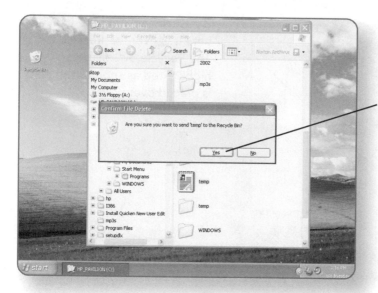

3. Press the **Delete** key. A dialog box will appear, asking if you are sure you want to send this item to the Recycle Bin.

4. Click Yes. The file will now be in the Recycle Bin.

Sending Files to the Recycle Bin with the Mouse

The Recycle Bin resides on the desktop and is represented by an icon with a recycle logo. By dragging files, folders, or icons onto that icon, you can send them to the Recycle Bin.

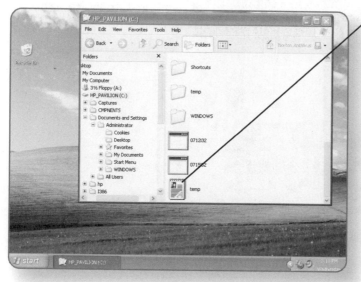

1. Position your **mouse pointer** over the **file, folder, or icon** that you want to send to the Recycle Bin.

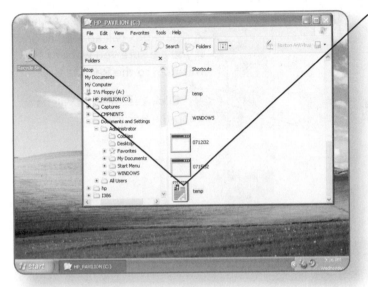

2. **Click** and **drag** the **icon** until it is over the Recycle Bin. The Recycle Bin will be highlighted as soon as the item is placed over it.

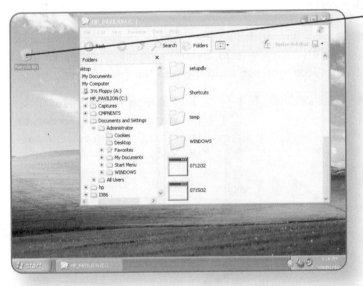

3. **Release** the **mouse button**. The file will be sent to the Recycle Bin. The Recycle Bin icon will appear to have a piece of paper in it, to indicate that it is not empty.

Viewing the Contents of the Recycle Bin

At its basic level, the Recycle Bin is simply a folder on your computer where deleted files are sent. At any time, you can view the contents of the Recycle Bin.

1. Double-click on the **Recycle Bin**. A window will open showing you all of the contents of the Recycle Bin.

2. Click the **x** in the top-right corner of the window to close the Recycle Bin.

Restoring Contents

The main point of having the Recycle Bin is as a second chance for files that you may have inadvertently deleted. Restoring files that have been sent to the Recycle Bin is just a matter of a few clicks of the mouse button.

1. **Double-click** on the **Recycle Bin**. A window will open showing you the contents of the Recycle Bin.

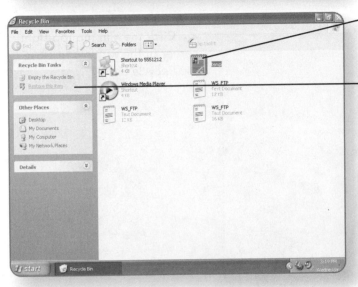

2. **Click** the **item** that you would like to restore. It will be highlighted, once selected.

3. **Click** the **Restore this item** link. The item will be restored to the location from where it was deleted.

TIP

You can restore the entire contents of the Recycle Bin by not selecting any items and clicking the Restore all items link.

Emptying the Recycle Bin

It's a good idea to occasionally empty the Recycle Bin so that unnecessary space isn't being used up. Once you've decided that you want to permanently remove an item or items from your computer, it's time to empty the Recycle Bin. Be sure that you want this item deleted, as once the Recycle Bin is emptied, the item can no longer be restored.

1. **Right-click** on the **Recycle Bin**. A menu will appear.

2. **Click Empty Recycle Bin**. The Confirm Multiple File Delete dialog box will appear.

3. **Click Yes**. The contents of the Recycle Bin will be permanently deleted.

Configuring the Recycle Bin

Using Windows XP Media Center Edition, you can control a variety of different settings for your Recycle Bin. Its size can be altered, and you can have it so that the Recycle Bin is automatically bypassed when deleting files.

Automatically Bypassing the Recycle Bin

If you're a person who knows what you want and don't like to be second-guessed, then the option is available to automatically bypass the Recycle Bin. In other words, the Recycle Bin gets turned into a garbage disposal where anything you put into it automatically gets deleted.

1. **Right-click** on the **Recycle Bin**. A menu will appear.

2. **Click Properties**. The Recycle Bin Properties dialog box will open.

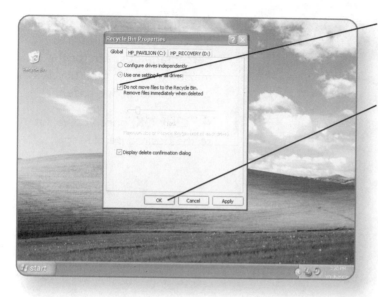

3. Click the **box** beside **Do not move files to the Recycle Bin**. Remove files immediately when deleted.

4. Click OK. The setting will take effect.

Changing the Size of the Recycle Bin

You can make your Recycle Bin super-strength industrial–sized, or it can be peewee shoebox-sized. The maximum size of your Recycle Bin is represented by a certain percentage of your hard drive space. You can limit or increase the size of the Recycle Bin by accessing its properties.

1. Right-click on the **Recycle Bin**. A menu will appear.

2. Click Properties. The Recycle Bin Properties dialog box will open.

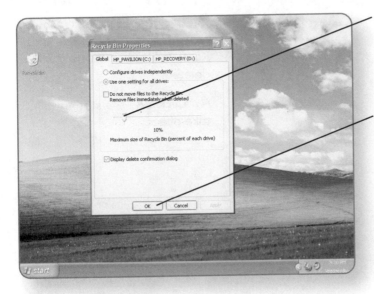

3. **Click** and **drag** the **slider bar** to the right or left. The percentage of space for the maximum size of the Recycle Bin will increase or decrease.

4. **Click OK**, once you've set it to the desired percentage.

14

Getting Help

Even seasoned computer professionals will occasionally need help when using the computer. If you're like most people, you probably only use about 15 percent of the total capabilities of your computer. This means that when it is time to perform a task that isn't routine, you might need a little help. Not to worry, Windows XP Media Center Edition is here to help. The operating system offers a variety of Help tools to help you with your computer experience. In this chapter, you'll learn how to:

- Search for help
- Access Help topics
- Obtain Remote Assistance
- Get help from Microsoft
- Take the Windows XP Tour

The Help and Support Center

The Help and Support Center holds most of the Help functionality within Windows XP Media Center Edition. It is your one-stop area to get answers to most of the questions that you might have when working with your computer.

1. **Click Start**. The Start menu will appear.

2. **Click Help and Support**. The Help and Support Center will open.

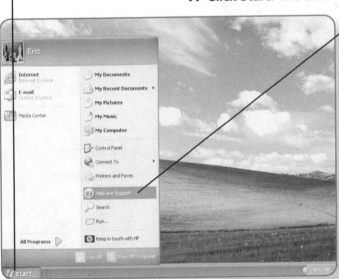

NOTE

Depending on who manufactured your computer, the Help and Support Center on your machine may look slightly different from the images you see here. Regardless of who manufactured your computer, the core functions of the Help and Support Center remain the same.

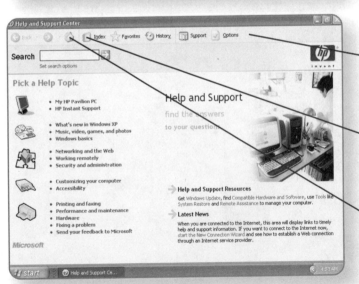

- **Toolbar.** The Toolbar allows you to navigate through the various Help pages that you visit.

- **Index.** This provides a window where you can browse through all of the different Help topics.

- **Home.** This button allows you to return to the main Help and Support Center page.

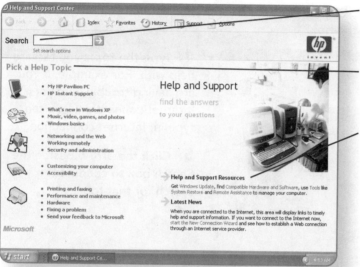

- **Search box.** The Search box allows you to search for help on specific topics.

- **Pick a Help Topic.** You can get help by selecting predefined Help topics.

- **Ask for Assistance.** This allows you to get support from others.

Searching for Help

One of the best ways to get help for a topic you are having trouble with is to use the Search function in the Help and Support Center.

1. Click Start. The Start menu will appear.

2. Click Help and Support. The Help and Support Center will open.

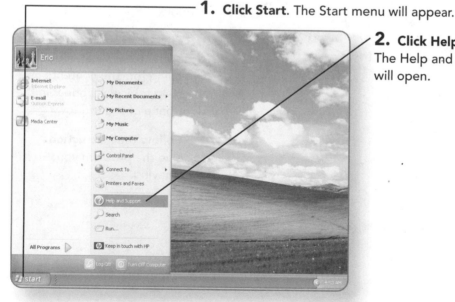

3. Click once in the **Search** box. Your cursor will be flashing in the box.

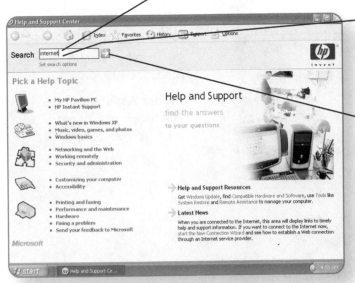

4. Type the **topic** you require help with. For example, if you are having trouble with your Internet connection, you can type in: Internet connection.

5. Click the **arrow** beside the Search box to conduct the search for that topic.

Results for your search will appear in the left pane of the window.

6. Click the **topic** that most closely matches what you were searching for. The contents of the Help topic will appear in the right pane of the window.

7. Follow the **instructions** to solve the problem you were having.

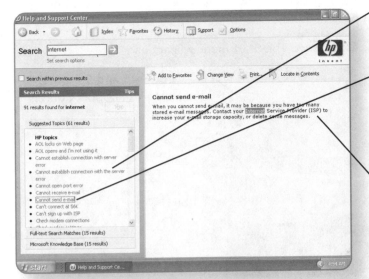

Using the Help Index

Rather than searching for a particular Help topic, you can browse through all of the Help keywords in the database to find help for the topic you are looking for.

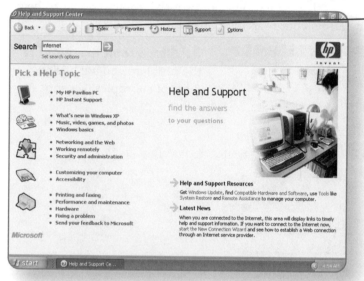

1. **Click** the **Index** button in the toolbar. The Index window will open, and all of the topics will be listed alphabetically in the window.

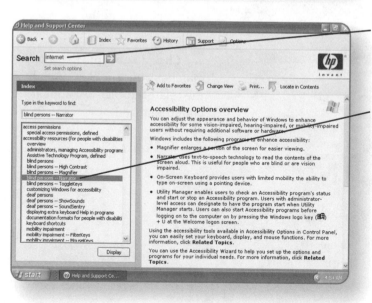

2. **Begin typing** the **keyword** of the topic you are looking for. As you type, any topics that match will be displayed.

3. **Double-click** on the **topic** that you would like to display. The information pertaining to that topic will be displayed in the right pane of the window.

Accessing the Help Topics

Windows XP Media Center Edition has a variety of Help topics in various categories to help you solve problems or answer questions that you may have. Using this method, each time you click on a topic, more specific topics appear to help you narrow your search for answers.

1. **Click** a **topic** that best fits the problem you are having. A list of subtopics will appear.

2. **Click** a **subtopic** that best matches your problem. All of the related topics will appear underneath.

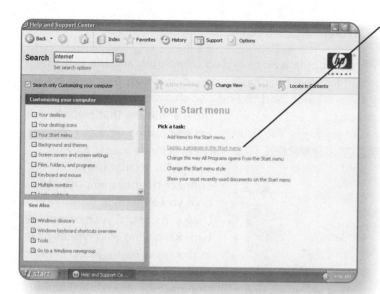

3. Click the appropriate **task** that covers your problem. Step-by-step instructions will appear.

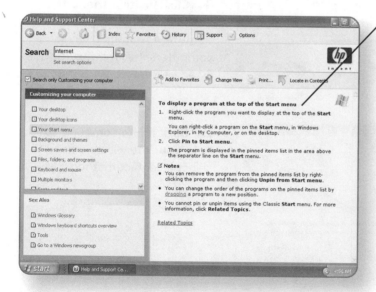

4. Follow the **instructions** to solve your problem.

Remote Assistance

With the popularity of desktop computing and the fact that computers have become ingrained in almost every aspect of our lives, it's not hard to find people who are experts in computing. If you happen to know someone that has a knack for computing, you can give them remote access to your computer so that they can connect to your computer and give you a hand. In other words, they can control your computer without having to physically be in the same room. Keep in mind that you must be connected to the Internet in order to use this feature.

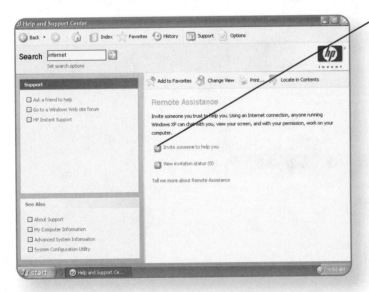

1. **Click Invite a friend to connect to your computer with Remote Assistance.** On some computers, this may just be listed as **Remote Assistance**.

2. **Click Invite someone to help you.** You will now have to select a contact method.

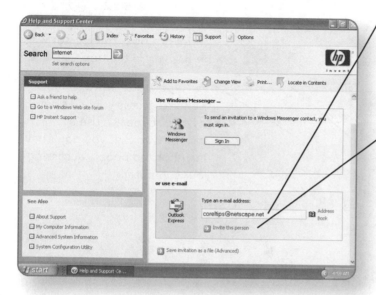

3. Type the **e-mail address** of the person you want to invite. Alternatively, you can use Windows Instant Messenger to invite a user, if you have an account set up.

4. Click Invite this person. You can now enter the text of your invitation.

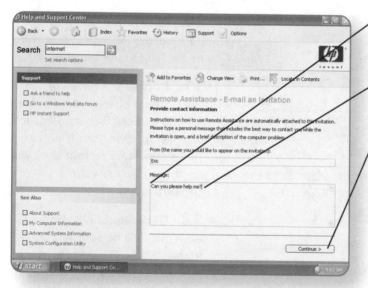

5. Click once in the **Message** area. Your cursor will be flashing.

6. Type in the **message**, inviting the user to gain access to your computer.

7. Click Continue. You will advance to the next screen, where you can enter a user name and password for your friend to access your computer.

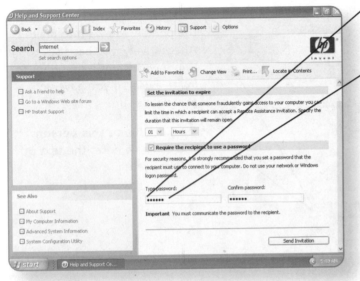

8. **Click** once in the **Type password** box. Your cursor will be flashing in the box.

9. **Type** a **password** for your friend to access your computer. It's a good idea to use a password so that you don't have unauthorized people accessing your computer.

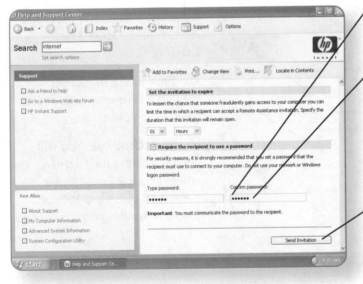

10. **Click** in the **Confirm password** box. Your cursor will be flashing in the box.

11. **Retype** the **password** in the Confirm password box. You will have to call or communicate the password to your friend in some other way so that they will be able to access your computer.

12. **Click Send Invitation**. An e-mail will be sent to your friend, letting them know you want assistance and giving them instructions for connecting to your computer.

Taking the Windows XP Tour

If you are a visual learner, you can sit back, relax, and watch the Windows XP Tour. The Tour covers a variety of topics from basics to advanced tips and tricks.

1. Click the **Start** button. The Start menu will appear.

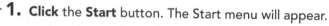

2. Click All Programs. A list of different programs and categories will appear.

3. Click Accessories. More programs and categories will appear.

4. Click Tour Windows XP. This will launch the Windows XP Tour.

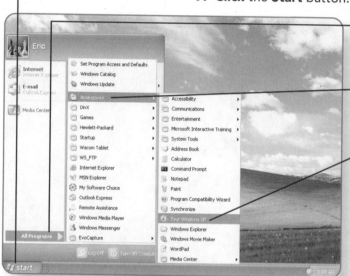

5. Click Next to begin the Tour.

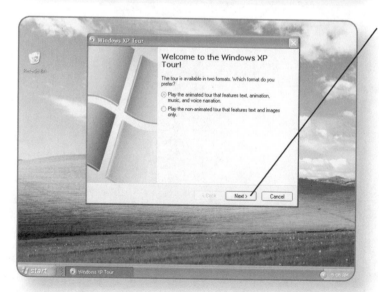

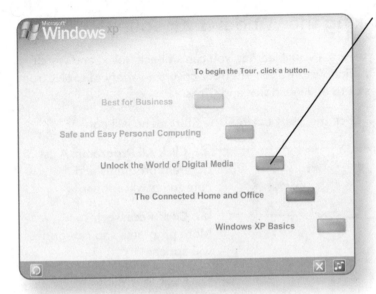

6. **Click** on the **topic** you'd like to watch. The Tour will continue.

15

Connecting to the Internet

There's a good likelihood that much of the time that you spend on your computer will be performing some online function like surfing the Internet, checking e-mail, or connecting to a network. Windows XP Media Center Edition does most of the work for you when it comes to setting up your Internet connection. If you are using a cable or high-speed modem, your connection should be automatically detected. For dial-up connections, there is a convenient wizard that will step you through connecting to the Internet. In this chapter, you'll learn how to:

- Run the New Connection Wizard
- Set up an Internet account
- Dial up to the Internet

The New Connection Wizard

The New Connection Wizard will help you connect to the Internet. Step by step, it will ask you questions pertaining to your connection. If you have a cable or high-speed modem that is always connected to the Internet, there is no need to run this wizard, as Windows XP Media Center Edition will automatically detect your connection. On the other hand, if you have dial-up access, it is a good idea to run through this wizard. You will need to have the dial-up number, your user name, and your password that your ISP (Internet Service Provider) assigned you.

1. **Click** the **Start** button. The Start menu will appear.

2. **Click All Programs**. A list of different programs will appear.

3. **Click Accessories**. A list of programs and categories will appear.

4. **Click Communications**. More programs will appear.

5. **Click New Connection Wizard**. The New Connection Wizard will launch.

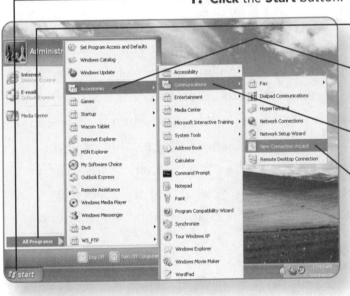

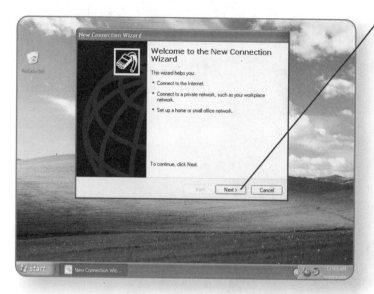

6. **Click Next** at the first screen to begin the setup process.

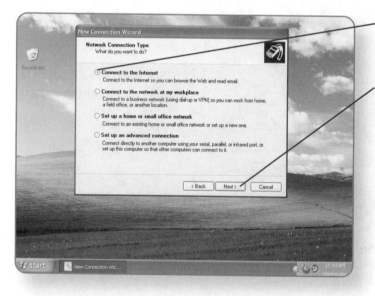

7. **Click** the **circle** beside Connect to the Internet, if it is not already selected.

8. **Click Next**. You'll advance to the next screen of the wizard.

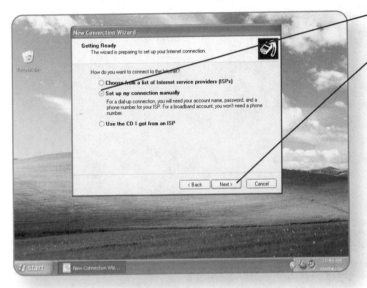

9. **Click** the **circle** beside Set up my connection manually.

10. **Click Next**. You'll advance to the next screen of the wizard.

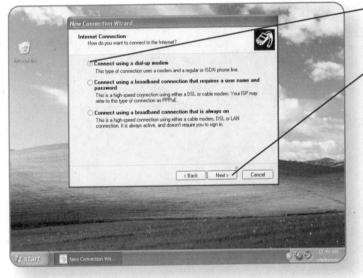

11. **Click** the **circle** beside Connect using a dial-up modem, if it is not already selected.

12. **Click Next**. You'll advance to the next screen of the wizard.

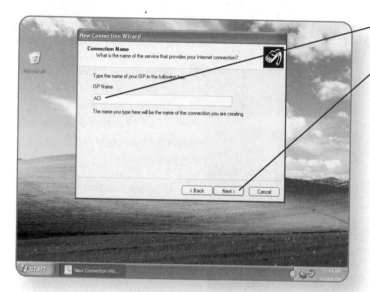

13. **Type** the **name** of your Internet Service Provider.

14. **Click Next**. You'll advance to the next screen of the wizard.

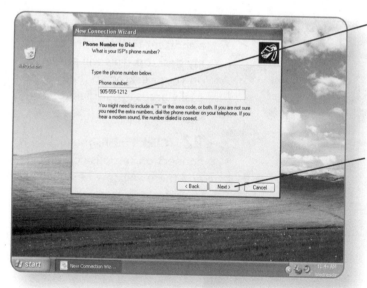

15. **Type** the **dial-up number**. Type it in as you would dial a number on your phone. For example, in your area, if you need to enter the area code first, then type the area code in first.

16. **Click Next**. You'll advance to the next screen of the wizard.

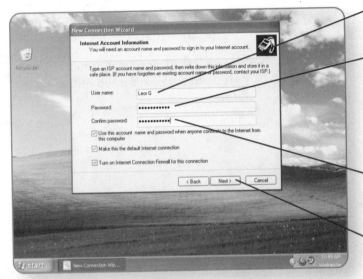

17. **Type** the **User name** that your ISP provided you with.

18. **Type** in the **Password** that your ISP provided you with. It will show up as a series of asterisks so that nobody watching the screen will see your password.

19. **Retype** the **Password** to confirm you've entered it correctly.

20. **Click Next**. You'll advance to the next screen of the wizard.

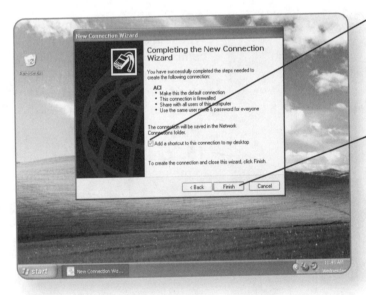

21. **Click** the **box** beside Add a shortcut to this connection to my desktop. This will put an icon on your desktop so that you can easily access your dial-up connection.

22. **Click Finish**. Your connection setup is complete, and there will now be an icon on your desktop that will allow you to dial up to the Internet.

Dialing Up to the Internet

Once you've set up your connection, you can now dial up to your ISP and start working online. You will need to dial up to the Internet every time you want to access e-mail, surf the Web, or connect to a network.

1. Click Start. The Start menu will appear.

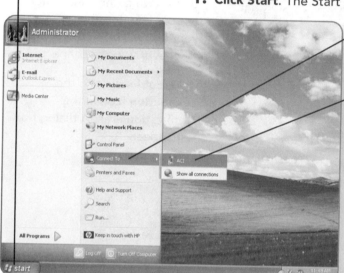

2. Click Connect To. Any connections that you have set up will appear.

3. Click your **connection**. The Connections dialog box will open.

TIP

If you set up a dial-up icon during the connection setup, you can double-click on it to launch the Connections dialog box.

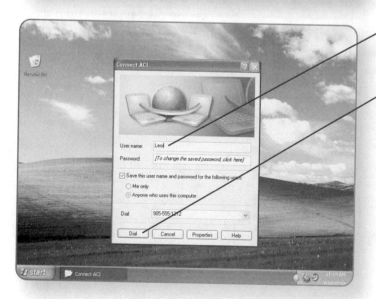

4. Type in your **User name** if it is not already filled in. Your ISP has provided this to you.

5. Click Dial. The computer will dial your ISP and you'll now be connected to the Internet.

Disconnecting from the Internet

Most dial-up Internet services offer you a certain number of hours per month. For this reason, it is a good idea to disconnect from the Internet when you are no longer using it. This is especially true if you don't have a dedicated phone line for your Internet access, as your line will be tied up whenever you are connected.

1. Double-click on the **connection icon** in the Notification area. A dialog box will appear.

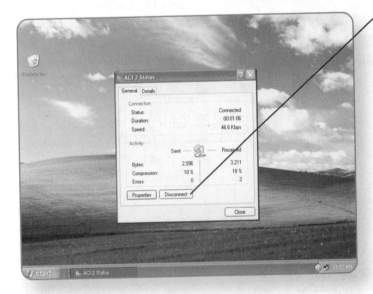

2. Click Disconnect. You will now be disconnected from the Internet.

16

Surfing the Internet with Internet Explorer

The wonderful world of the Internet is at your fingertips. Search engines, chat rooms, online newspapers, banking, job sites, and so much more are yours to discover. Your Windows XP Media Center Edition computer comes with several different ways to surf the Net, but the most popular by far is Internet Explorer. The Internet is made of pages, typically created in HTML, the language of the Internet. Internet Explorer and other programs like it read HTML pages and present them for you to view. In this chapter, you'll learn how to:

- Browse the Web with Internet Explorer
- Search Web sites
- Access your favorite sites
- Customize Internet Explorer

Launching Internet Explorer

Before you launch Internet Explorer, you have to ensure that you are connected to the Internet. If you are using a dial-up connection, make sure you have followed the steps from the chapter on connecting to the Internet and have initiated your connection before you launch Internet Explorer. If you are using a cable connection that has already been configured, you needn't do any prep work.

1. **Click** the **Start** button. The Start menu will appear.

2. **Click All Programs**. A list of programs and program categories will appear.

3. **Click Internet Explorer**. Internet Explorer will launch.

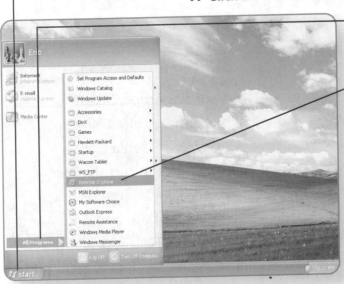

Getting to Know Internet Explorer

The various parts of the Internet Explorer window will make your Internet surfing experience easier. Every toolbar can be turned off or on, depending on your personal preference.

1. **Click View.** A menu will appear.

2. **Click Toolbars** and a submenu will appear.

3. **Click** on the **Toolbar** option you'd like to turn on or off. Those with a check mark beside them are already turned on.

- **Toolbar.** Provides you with the common navigation tools for surfing the Internet.

- **Links bar.** The Tab bar allows you to surf multiple pages at one time, without having to open a separate Internet Explorer window.

- **Address bar.** You can access frequently visited sites using this toolbar.

- **Status bar.** Provides you with information on the site that you are visiting. Typically, this includes the name of the site and the percentage of the site that has been loaded.

Entering Web Addresses

Every page on the Internet has a specific address. You have to let Internet Explorer know what address you are looking for, and it will search the Web, find the address, and load it into the window viewing area. The nice part is that Internet Explorer is a pretty fast worker, as all of those tasks can usually be accomplished in a matter of seconds.

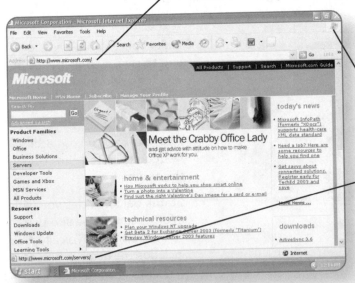

1. Double-click in an area of the Address bar. All of the text will be highlighted so that, when you begin to type, it will disappear.

2. Type in the **URL address** of the site that you'd like to visit. For example, www.premierpressbooks.com.

3. Press the **Enter** key. Internet Explorer will begin looking for the Web page.

4. Watch the **Internet Explorer logo**. If the flag stops waving, it means that Internet Explorer is working on finding your site.

5. Monitor the **Status bar**, as it will indicate how much of your Web page has been loaded.

Using Hyperlinks

Almost every Web page includes hyperlinks that allow you to jump from one page to another without having to type out the address in the Address bar. Typically, you can tell a hyperlink from any other picture or text because the text is underlined and in the color blue, or more accurately, your cursor will change to a little hand when it is over a hyperlink.

1. Position your **mouse pointer** over a **hyperlink**. It will change to a little hand if it is over a hyperlink.

2. Click on the **hyperlink**. The Web page will be loaded into the window.

Moving Backward and Forward

Internet Explorer provides you with an easy way to go back and forth through pages that you have previously visited.

1. Click the **Back** button. The page that you previously visited will now appear in the Viewer window.

2. Click the **Forward** button. The page you had just come back from will now appear.

TIP

To go back or forward several pages, you don't need to continuously click the Back or Forward buttons. Beside each button there is a little arrow. By clicking on the arrow, a list will appear of the last Web pages you visited. You can simply click on one of those pages and you will be advanced there.

Searching the Web

There are literally millions of Web pages on the Internet, so the task of finding the specific information you need may sometimes seem like looking for the proverbial needle in a haystack. There are many different search Web sites that can help you, but Internet Explorer actually has a Search function built in.

1. Double-click in a **blank area** of the Address bar to highlight the text.

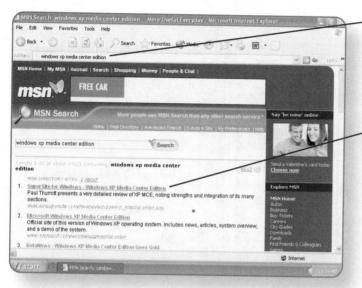

2. Type in the **keywords** that you are looking for.

3. Press Enter. MSN will conduct a search and display the results.

4. Click on the **desired result**. You will be taken to the site you've clicked.

TIP

If you enter more than one keyword, you may want to put a quotation mark before them. Preceding your keyword with a quotation mark will yield results that match those keywords exactly. Without the quotations, the search will be conducted showing results that match any or all of the keywords. For example, if you searched for Dallas Cowboys, the search results would include any site that matched the word Dallas or Cowboys or Dallas Cowboys. If you had entered "Dallas Cowboys," only sites that matched those two words in that order would be searched.

Finding Text

Sometimes Web pages are designed in such a way that there is a mountain of information being displayed, and you can't seem to find the specific thing you're looking for. Internet Explorer has a built-in search function that will allow you to find instances of specific text on that page.

1. Click Edit. The Edit menu will appear.

2. Click Find (on This Page). A dialog box will now appear where you can enter your search criteria.

TIP

Clicking Ctrl+F will open the Find dialog box.

3. Type the **text** you are looking for.

You can also set certain parameters in this dialog box, like match the case, match the whole word, or search up or down.

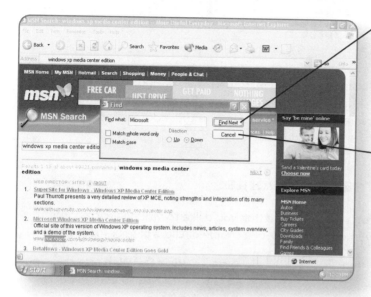

4. **Click Find Next**. If the text you are looking for is found, it will be highlighted.

5. **Click Find Next again** to jump to the next instance of the text.

6. **Click Cancel** to close the dialog box.

Refresh

The Internet is always changing. In fact, some pages will change every few seconds. Let's say, for example, you are visiting a Web site that provided you with the price of a stock. As the stock price is always changing, what you view as a certain price may be changing as you are visiting the site. Rather than having to type in the URL address again, you can reload the data to see any updated changes. This tool is also useful if a page isn't loading correctly or if you can't see the graphics properly.

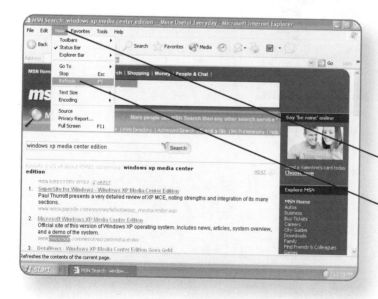

1. **Click View**. A menu will appear.

2. **Click Refresh**. The information on the Web page will be reloaded, and any updates can now be seen.

TIP

Pressing F5 will also refresh your page.

Favorites

There is no doubt that you'll come across Web pages that you will want to visit again. Rather than having to grab a pen and jot down the address, you can "Favorites" it within Internet Explorer. Favorites will save the URL address for you so that it can be accessed later.

Creating Favorites

If you've found a site that you'd like to visit again, creating Favorites is a matter of a couple of clicks of your mouse button.

1. Visit the **Web site** that you want to add to your list of Favorites.

2. Click Favorites. The Favorites menu will now appear.

3. Click Add to Favorites. A dialog box will appear confirming that you want to add this page to your Favorites list.

4. Click OK. The page will be added to your Favorites list.

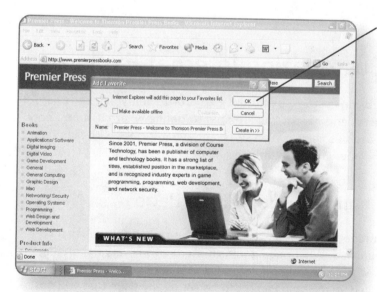

TIP

Press Ctrl+D when you are visiting any Web site and it will be added to your Favorites list.

Accessing Favorites

Once you have added some Web pages to your Favorites list, you can access them through the Favorites menu.

1. Click Favorites. The Favorites menu will appear.

2. Click the **desired Web site** from the list and that page will be loaded into the viewer.

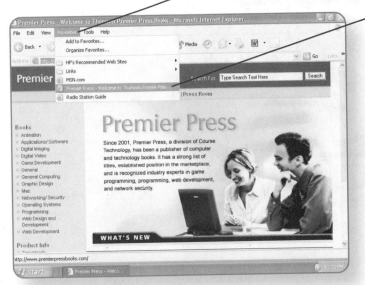

Customizing Internet Explorer

You can customize Internet Explorer to suit your particular tastes and needs. You are able to define where it starts, how it handles certain Web sites, and what it does with files that you have downloaded.

Changing Your Home Page

Internet Explorer always starts at a specific page when it is launched. What page it initially starts at will vary depending on how your Internet Explorer was first configured. This page, called your Home Page, can be set to any page that you desire.

1. Click Tools. The Tools menu will appear.

2. Click Internet Options. This will open up the Internet Options dialog box that will allow you to change your Home Page.

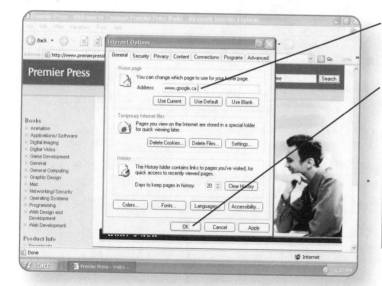

3. Type the **URL** of the page you'd like to have as your Home Page.

4. Click OK. Your new Home Page has now been set.

TIP

You can get back to your Home Page at any time by clicking on the Home button in the toolbar.

Adding and Removing Links

You can add your own buttons to the Links toolbar to go one step further than just using Favorites. If you have a Web site that you visit often, you can save the steps of typing in the URL address or accessing Favorites. By using the Links toolbar, you can create a button that will take you to that site whenever you click on it. Typically, the Links toolbar starts off as locked, so you must first unlock and position it, and then it can be customized.

1. Right-click on the word **Links**. A menu will appear.

2. Click Lock the Toolbars. This will actually unlock the toolbar so that it can be repositioned.

3. Position your **mouse pointer** over the word **Links**.

4. Click and **drag downward** slightly. Your cursor will change into a four-sided arrow, and the toolbar will be previewed in its new position.

5. Release the **mouse button**. The Links toolbar will be repositioned.

6. Visit the **Web site** that you want to create a button for on your Personal toolbar.

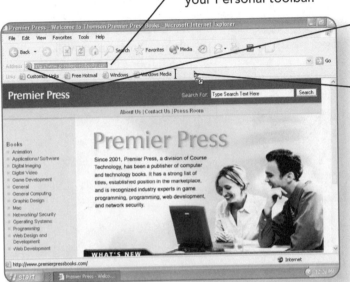

7. Position the **mouse pointer** over the **icon** to the left of the URL address in the Address bar.

8. Click and **drag** to an **empty area** of the Links toolbar. As you are dragging, the mouse pointer will change. When your cursor is over the Links toolbar, a little line will appear.

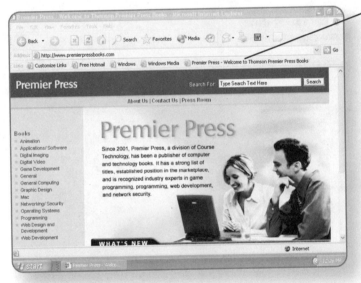

9. Release the **mouse button** when you are over the Personal toolbar. A button representing that site will now appear on the Personal toolbar.

10. Right-click on the **button** that you would like to rename. A menu will appear.

11. Click Rename. A dialog box will appear where you can rename the button.

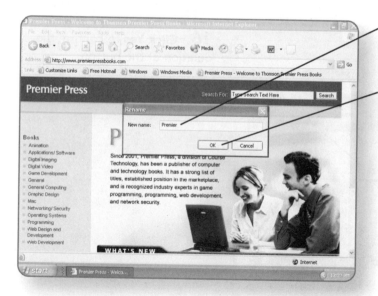

12. Type the **desired name**. You can give your button any name you choose.

13. Click OK. The button will be renamed.

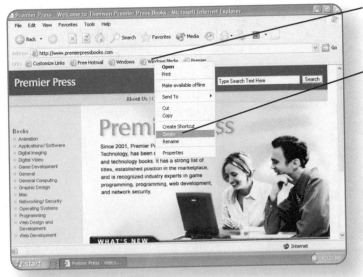

14. **Right-click** on the **button** that you would like to remove. A menu will appear.

15. **Click Delete**. A dialog box will appear.

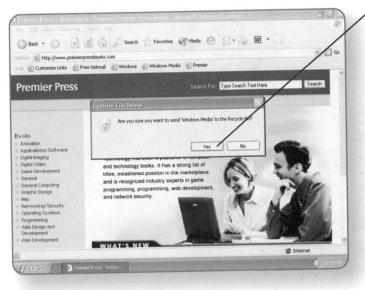

16. **Click Yes** to confirm the deletion of the button.

17

E-Mailing with Outlook Express

Remember the days of actually writing a letter, putting a stamp on it, and waiting a week or two for a reply? With the emergence of electronic mail, those days are all but forgotten. Nowadays, you can send an e-mail, it will almost instantly arrive in the recipient's mailbox, and—once they send you a response—it usually arrives in seconds. There are a variety of free Web-based e-mail services that allow you to send and receive e-mails using your Web browser. If you want more advanced e-mail functionality, Windows XP Media Center Edition comes with an excellent e-mail program called Outlook Express. In this chapter, you'll learn how to:

- Set up Outlook Express
- Create and format e-mails
- Receive e-mails
- Manage your e-mails

Outlook Express

In order for Outlook Express to work properly, you will need to ensure that you have access to the Internet through a modem or some other Internet connection.

1. Click Start. The Start menu will appear.

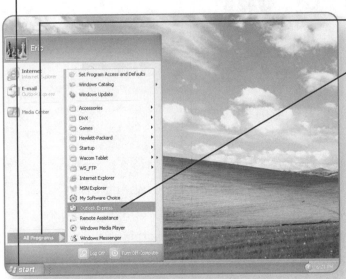

2. Click All Programs. A list of programs will appear.

3. Click Outlook Express. Outlook Express will be launched.

E-Mail Setup

Before you get started in setting up Outlook Express, you will require some information from your Internet Service Provider (ISP). You'll need to know the e-mail address they've given you, the incoming mail server, and the outgoing mail server. Once you have this information, you are ready to start configuring your e-mail. When you start Outlook Express for the first time, an Account Wizard dialog box will appear to take you step by step through the configuration process.

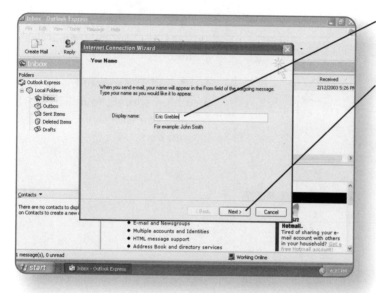

1. Type your Display name. This is the name that people will see when you send them e-mail.

2. Click Next. You'll be forwarded to the next screen of the wizard, where you'll enter your e-mail address.

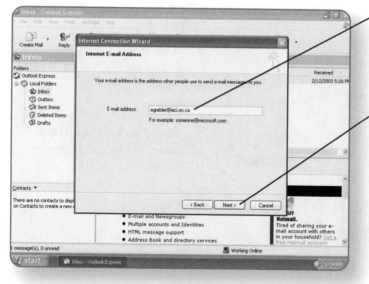

3. Type your **e-mail address**. This is the address that your ISP provided you with. Typically, it is in the form of yourname@yourisp.com.

4. Click Next. You will now be prompted for your e-mail server information.

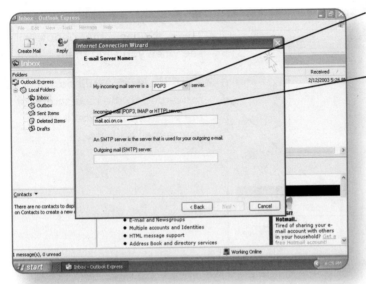

5. **Click** in the **Incoming mail server** box. Your cursor will flash in the box.

6. **Type** the **name** of the **Incoming server**. Your ISP can provide you with this information.

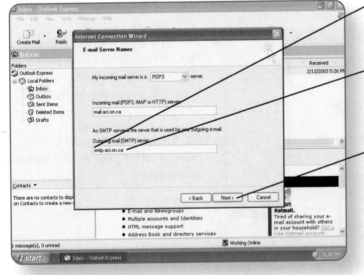

7. **Click** in the **Outgoing mail server** box. Your cursor will flash in the box.

8. **Type** the **name** of the **Outgoing server**. Your ISP can provide you with this information.

9. **Click Next**. You will be advanced to the next page in the wizard.

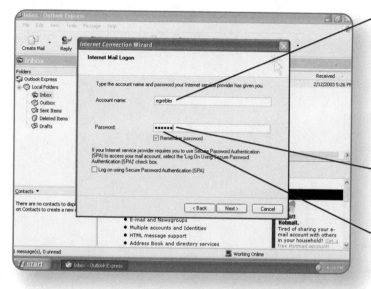

10. **Type** in the **Account name**. This is the account name that your ISP provided you with. Typically, it's the first part of your e-mail. For example, if your e-mail address was robblier@e-mail.com your account name would most likely be robblier.

11. **Click** in the **Password** box. The cursor will be flashing in the box.

12. **Type** the **password** that your ISP provided you. It will appear as a series of asterisks.

Un-checking the Remember password box means that you will have to enter your password every time you launch your e-mail program.

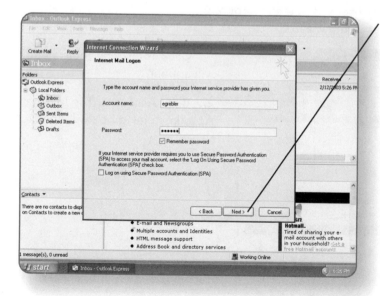

13. **Click Next**. You will be advanced to the next page in the wizard.

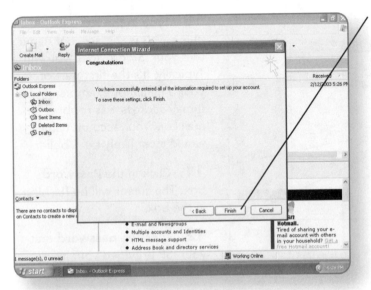

14. **Click Finish** after reviewing that all of the settings are correct.

Launching the Wizard

If for some reason the New Account wizard doesn't open the first time you launch Outlook Express, or if you want to add a new user to the e-mail program, you can always manually launch the wizard.

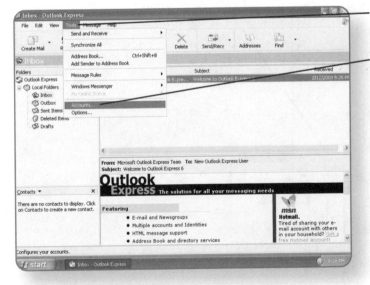

1. **Click Tools**. The Tools menu will appear.

2. **Click Accounts**. The Internet Accounts dialog box will open.

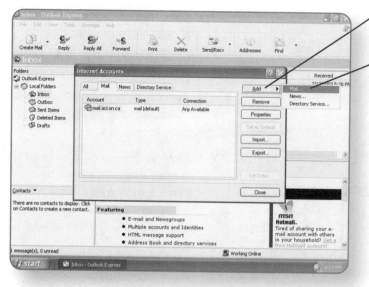

3. Click Add. A list of options will appear.

4. Click Mail. The wizard will launch.

Getting to Know the Mail Program

Now that the mail program is configured, it's time to get to know the main parts of the screen that you'll be working with.

When you open Outlook Express, you are greeted by a Welcome screen that indicates if you have any new unread messages.

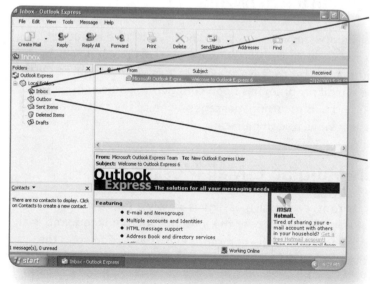

1. Click Inbox. The Inbox will open, showing you any e-mail you may have received.

- **Inbox.** This is essentially your mailbox. When someone sends you an e-mail, it initially goes to your inbox.

- **Outbox.** The Outbox stores all of the messages that you want to send. Typically, messages go in the Outbox when you are offline. Once you are online, the messages will be sent.

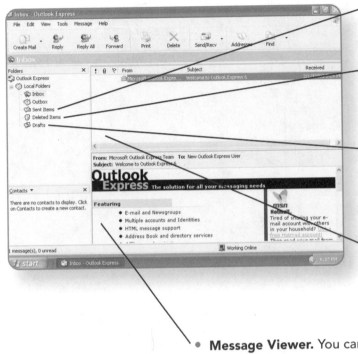

- **Sent Items.** This folder keeps a copy of any e-mail messages that you have sent.

- **Deleted Items.** Similar to the Recycle Bin on your computer, this folder stores deleted e-mails until it is emptied.

- **Drafts.** When you create an e-mail, you don't have to send it right away. Unfinished or unsent e-mails can be stored in the Drafts folder.

- **Information Viewer.** This area lets you view your messages at a glance, including who sent you a message and what its subject was.

- **Message Viewer.** You can view the actual contents of your e-mail in this area.

Sending E-Mails

No stamps, no envelopes, and no licking—the beauty of electronic mail. You can send e-mails anytime and anywhere without having to leave the comfort of your computer. Once the e-mail program has been configured, you can begin sending and receiving messages—one of the fastest and easiest ways to communicate.

Creating an E-Mail Message

At its root, an e-mail message is simply a text message that you send someone over the Internet. All that is required is an e-mail address so the computer knows where to send the message and, of course, the message itself.

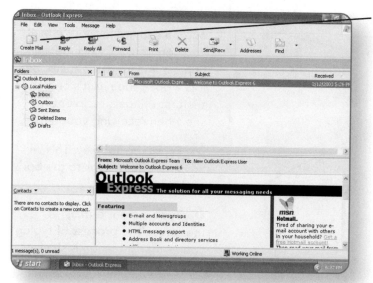

1. Click on the **Create Mail** button. This will open up a dialog box where you can create your message.

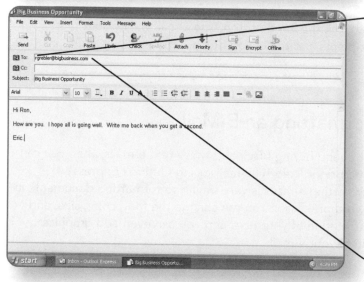

2. Click in the **To:** section of the dialog box. Your cursor will be flashing in the box.

TIP

If you want to send a carbon copy of the e-mail you are sending to another recipient, you can click in the Cc: box and type in their e-mail address.

3. Type the **e-mail address** of the person you wish to send the message to. Typically, it's in the form name@isp.com.

TIP

If you are sending e-mail to more than one recipient, you can put a comma or a semicolon in between their e-mail addresses.

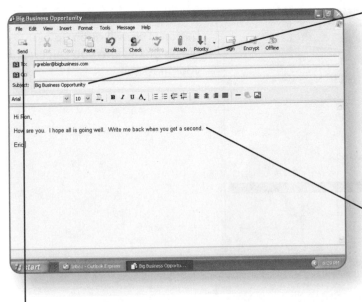

4. **Click** in the **Subject** line to enter a subject for your e-mail. You don't have to include a Subject line in your e-mails, but it is a good idea as it's one of the first things a recipient will see when receiving your e-mail.

5. **Press** the **Tab** key. This will advance your cursor to the body of the message.

6. **Type** in your **e-mail message**. The process of typing your e-mail message is similar to that of typing in a word processor.

7. **Click** the **Send** button. The e-mail will be sent to its recipients and the dialog box will close.

Formatting an E-Mail

Why send boring black-and-white text e-mails when you can send bright, colorful e-mails using Outlook Express? Formatting e-mails is very similar to formatting documents in a word processor. You can change the font, color, size, and justification of your text, and you can even add graphics within your e-mail.

Formatting Text

If you've ever used a word processor, then formatting text in an e-mail should seem very familiar to you.

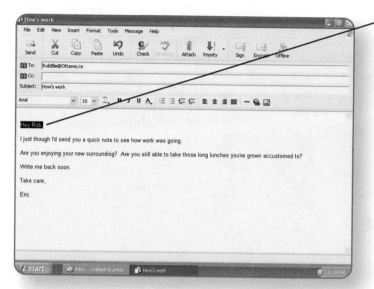

1. **Click** and **drag** across the **text** that you'd like to add a heading to. A heading is a preset format that you can apply to a body of text.

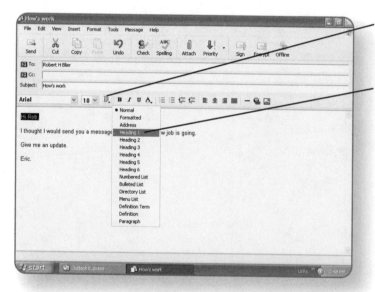

2. **Click** the **Paragraph Style** button to choose from a list of different heading styles.

3. **Select** the **desired paragraph style**. The formatting of the selected text will change.

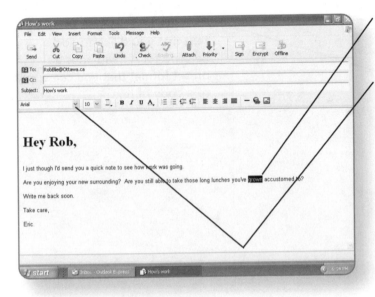

4. Click and **drag** across the **text** you want to change. It will become highlighted.

5. Click on the **down arrow** beside the font name. A list of fonts will appear.

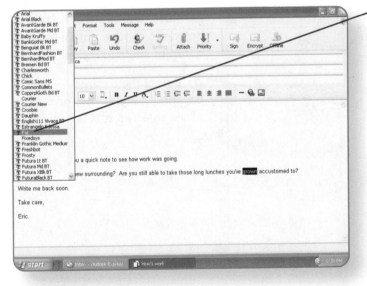

6. Select the **desired font**, and the highlighted text will now change to that font.

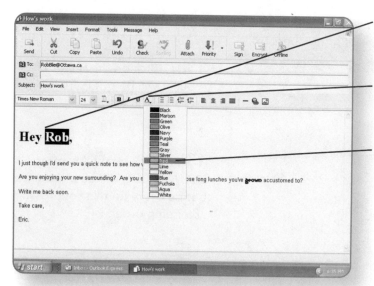

7. Click and **drag** across the **text** that you'd like to change color.

8. Click on the **Font Color** button. A list of different colors will appear.

9. Click the **desired color**.

10. Click and **drag** across the **text** that you'd like to modify.

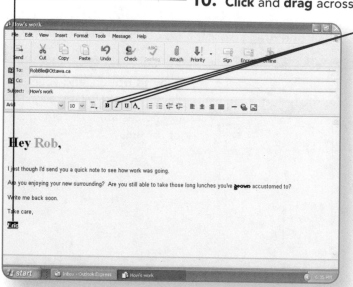

11. Select the **Bold**, **Italic**, or **Underline** buttons to apply those effects to the text.

TIP

The shortcut keys for Bold, Italic, and Underline are Ctrl+B, Ctrl+I, and Ctrl+U, respectively.

12. **Click** and **drag** across the **text** that you'd like to add bullets or numbers to.

13a. **Click** on the **Bullet List**. A bullet will be put in front of every item in the list.

OR

13b. **Click** on the **Number List**. Numbers will be placed beside every item in your list in ascending order.

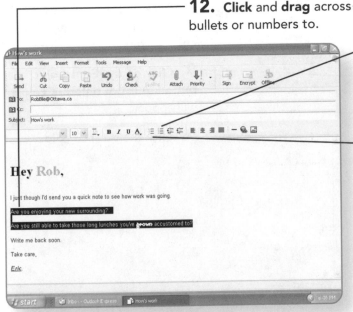

14. **Click** and **drag** across the **text** that you'd like to align.

15. **Select** the **desired alignment** option, and your highlighted text will be aligned. Your choices are left, center, right, or full.

Inserting Pictures into E-Mail

One of the great features of e-mail is that you can insert a picture directly into the body of your e-mail. Inserting pictures is different from attaching a picture, which we'll cover in the latter part of this chapter. Inserting puts the image directly in the body of the message, while attaching sends along a separate file.

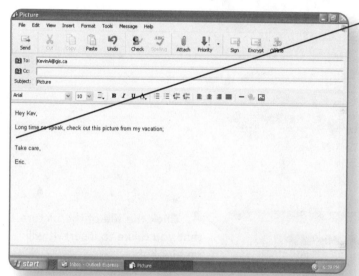

1. Click once where you want to insert a picture. The cursor will flash at that point.

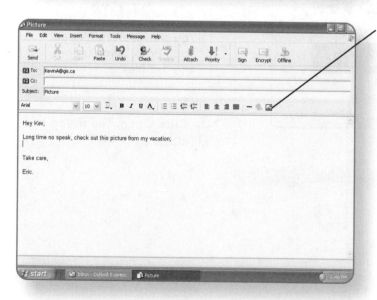

2. Click the **Insert Picture** button to open up a dialog box that will allow you to select an image.

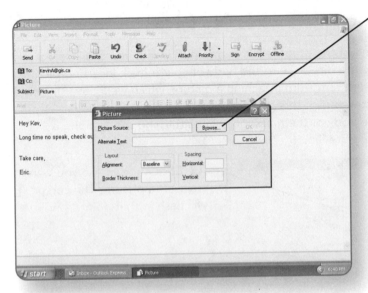

3. Click the **Browse** button. A dialog box will open, allowing you to select the location and file of your picture.

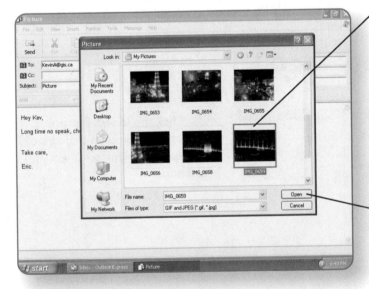

4. Click the **file** of the picture that you'd like to insert. It will be highlighted.

NOTE

You can insert .gif, .jpeg, .jpg, .bmp, .wmf, .xbm, and .art files.

5. Click Open. The dialog box will close.

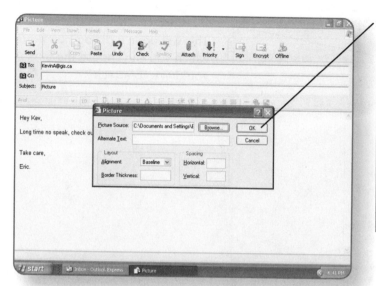

6. Click OK. The picture will be inserted into the e-mail.

Attaching Files to an E-Mail Message

A convenient way to send digital photos, documents, or other types of files to people is as an attachment. An attachment can be any file on your computer that you wish to share with someone else. You should keep in mind, however, that depending on your ISP (Internet Service Provider), there are certain limitations on the number and size of files that you can send in any one e-mail.

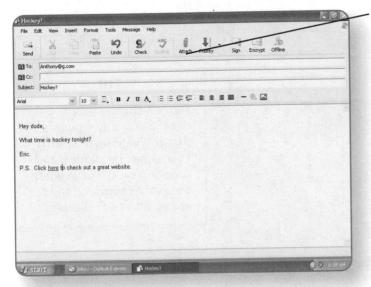

1. **Click** the **Attach** button. This will open a dialog box from which you can choose the file you'd like to attach.

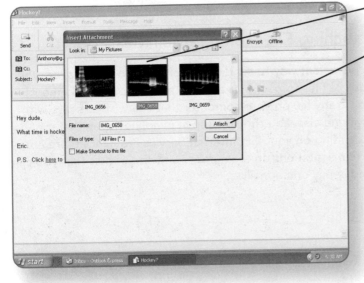

2. **Locate** and **click** the **file** that you'd like to attach.

3. **Click** the **Attach** button. This will attach the file to your e-mail.

Retrieving Incoming Messages

In my neighborhood, the mail carrier no longer comes to my door to deliver letters to the mailbox on my door. Instead, I have to walk half a block to a common mailbox, dealing with the rain, snow, sleet, and hail that were once only the enemies of the mail carrier. Fortunately, that's not the case with e-mail.

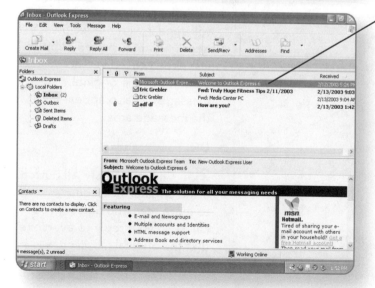

When someone sends you an e-mail message, it is delivered directly to the Inbox on your computer where it can be easily retrieved.

New Messages will appear in bold in your Information Viewer. When you open Outlook Express, it informs you of the number of new unread messages you have in your mailbox.

1. Click Inbox. The Inbox will open and all of the new messages will appear in bold in the Information Viewer.

2. Click on the **message** to view it. The contents of the message will appear in the Message area.

TIP

By double-clicking on a message, it will open in its own separate window.

Replying to an E-Mail Message

After you've read a message, you have the opportunity to respond to it by using the Reply command.

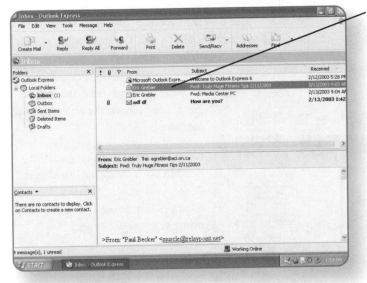

1. Click on the **message** that you want to reply to. Once selected, it will be highlighted.

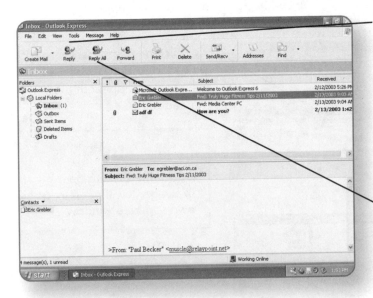

2a. Click the **Reply** button from the toolbar. A dialog box will appear with the recipient's e-mail address and the Subject line already filled in. The contents of the original message will also appear in the message area.

OR

2b. Click the **Reply All** button. If the original message was sent to more than one person, you can send your reply to everyone that the original message was sent to by clicking Reply All.

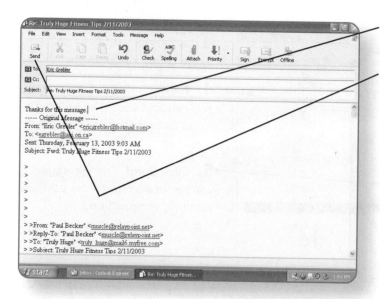

3. **Enter** the **text** of your message.

4. **Click** the **Send** button and your reply will be sent.

Forwarding a Message

If someone's sent you a juicy piece of gossip, you can keep the grapevine going by forwarding the message to someone else. When you forward a message that you've received to someone else, you can add your own message to send along with it. Any attachments in the original message will also be forwarded.

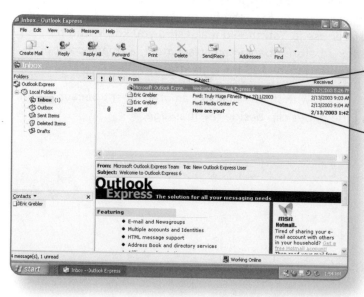

1. **Click** the **message** that you'd like to forward. It will now be highlighted.

2. **Click** the **Forward** button. The compose dialog box will appear, with the forwarded message in the body.

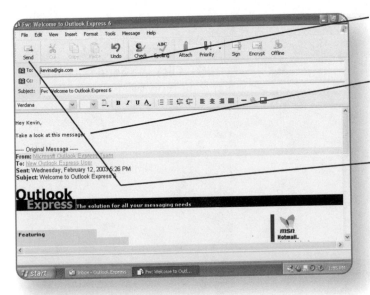

3. Type in the **e-mail address** of the person you'd like to forward this message to.

4. Type the **desired message**. You can add your own message to go along with the forwarded message.

5. Click Send. The message will be forwarded to the address that you've specified.

Working with Attachments

When someone sends you an e-mail with an attachment, you have several options as to what you can do with that attachment, including printing it, opening it, or saving it. In most cases, you'll save the file to your computer so that you can later use it. You should make sure you know who the sender is before opening an attachment, as many computer viruses are transmitted through attached files.

You will know that an e-mail has an attachment because there is a little paper clip beside the message.

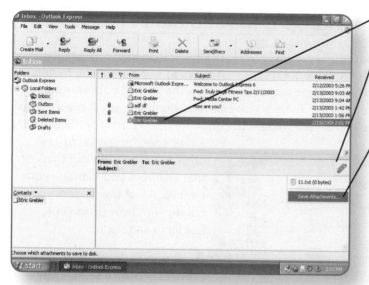

1. **Click** on a **message** to select it.

2. **Click** on the **Paper clip** button. A list of the attachments to this e-mail will appear.

3. **Click Save Attachments**. A dialog box will open.

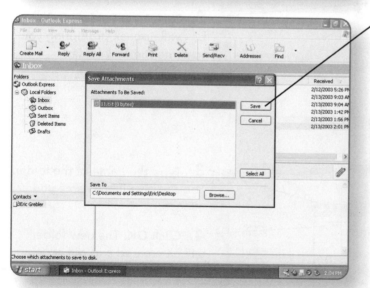

4. **Click Save**. The attachment will be saved to the location specified in this dialog box.

Managing Your E-Mail

Remember when you first started to get letters in the mail how exciting it was? Now you might dread going to your mailbox because it's filled with junk mail, bills, and other nonsense that you don't want, don't need, or would prefer not to get. The Mail application provides you with a variety of options for managing your e-mail.

Setting Up E-Mail Folders

Another way to help you manage your e-mail is to create specific folders for different types of e-mails. E-mail folders work the same way as folders on the rest of your computer. The types of folders you create are entirely at your discretion. You can create folders to contain e-mails from specific people, about specific topics, or any other way that you can think of that will help you manage your e-mails. All of the folders you create will show up in your Folders window.

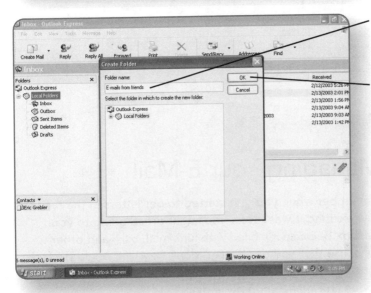

1. Right-click on **Local Folders**. A menu will appear.

2. Click New Folder. A dialog box will appear, prompting you to name the new folder.

3. Type the **name** of the folder. You can give it any name you choose.

4. Click OK. The new folder will be created and will appear in your folder list.

Deleting Messages

Once you have finished reading a message and have decided that you don't want to keep it in any of your folders, it can be deleted.

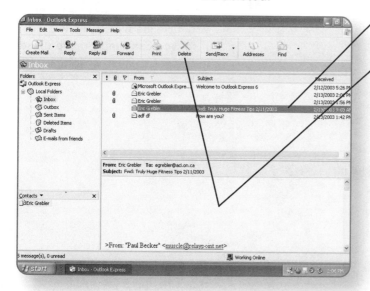

1. Click on the **message** that you want to delete.

2. Click the **Delete** button and the message will be moved to the Deleted Items folder.

Emptying the Deleted Items Folder

Just as when you delete files off of your computer, deleted e-mails can be found and restored from the e-mail Deleted Items folder. It acts as a safety net so that you don't inadvertently delete a message. It's a good idea to periodically empty out this folder, as the messages will start taking up valuable space on your computer's hard drive.

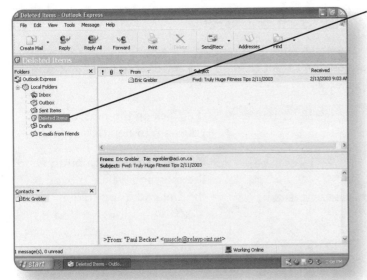

1. Click on the **Deleted Items** folder in the Folders window. This will display all of the messages that you have deleted. You can then determine if there are any messages that you have inadvertently deleted. If so, you can simply move those messages to another folder.

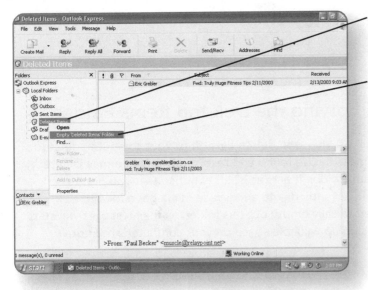

2. Right-click on the Deleted Items folder. A menu will appear.

3. Click Empty 'Deleted Items' Folder. A dialog box will appear, asking if you are sure you want to permanently delete these files.

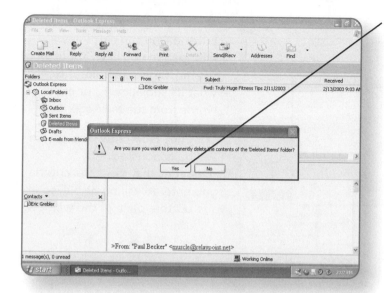

4. Click Yes. The contents of the Deleted Items folder will now be permanently removed.

Finding Messages

Once you've accumulated quite a few messages, finding one in particular may become difficult. The E-mail program has a built-in Search function that will allow you to search by sender or by subject name.

1. Click Edit. A menu will appear.

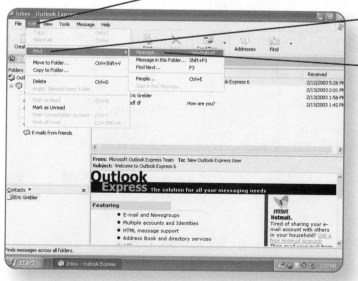

2. Click Find. A submenu will appear.

3. Click Message. A dialog box will open, allowing you to enter your search criteria.

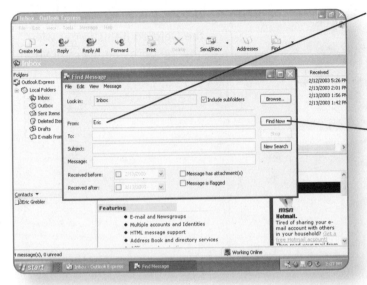

4. Type the **desired search criteria**. You can enter any information you have about who the message was from or to, what its subject was, or any words from the message itself.

5. Click **Find Now.** The search will be conducted. Any messages that meet the criteria you entered will be displayed in the bottom pane of the window.

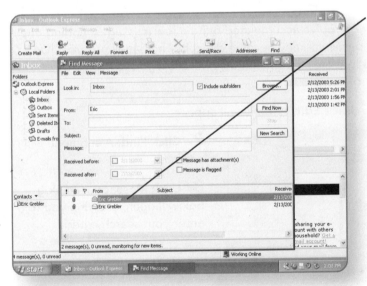

6. **Double-click** on the **desired result**. The message will open in a separate window.

18

Windows Messenger

Rather than having to wait for people to open their e-mail package, read the message, and send a reply, Windows XP Media Center Edition offers you a free, faster way to communicate by using Windows Messenger. With Windows Messenger, you can conduct an online conversation with a friend, relative, or coworker, or you can create or join a chat room where multiple people can participate. In this chapter, you'll learn how to:

- Set up Windows Messenger
- Send and receive messages
- Warn and block users

Launching Windows Messenger

Windows Messenger is an online communication tool, so in order for it to run properly, you must first be connected to the Internet. Windows Messenger can be accessed through the Start menu.

1. **Click Start**. The Start menu will appear.

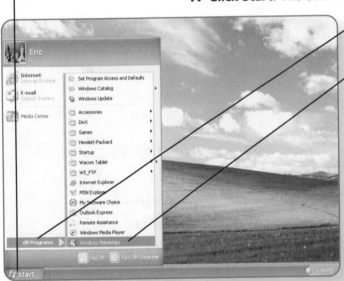

2. **Click All Programs**. A menu will appear.

3. **Click Windows Messenger**. The program will launch.

Setting Up a Windows Messenger Account

The first time you open Windows Messenger, you will need to set up your account. By setting up an account, you will create an address for yourself so that people can contact you when you are running Windows Messenger. When you set up an account, you will also be giving yourself access to other Microsoft .NET services.

1. **Click here to sign in.** This will launch the wizard.

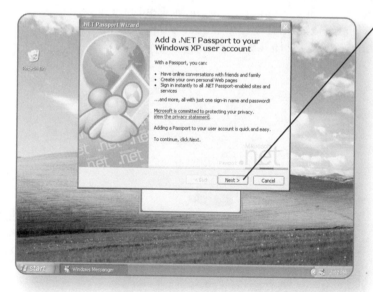

2. **Click Next**. The wizard will begin asking you questions pertinent to setting up your account.

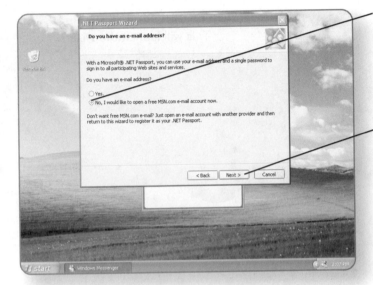

3. **Click** the **circle** beside No. It's a good idea to set up a separate e-mail for your .NET Passport, so even if you have an e-mail address, you should still select No.

4. **Click Next** to advance to the next screen of the wizard.

The wizard will now step you through the rest of the procedure for setting up an account. Continue entering information that the wizard requests until it is finished, and your account will be established.

Signing In to Windows Messenger

Once you launch Windows Messenger, it automatically remembers your password and logs you on whenever you are logged on to your computer.

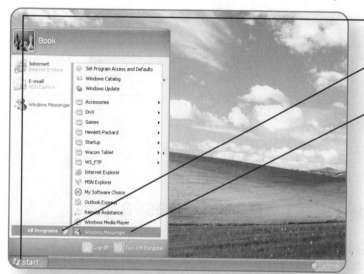

1. **Click Start**. The Start menu will appear.

2. **Click All Programs**. A menu will appear.

3. **Click Windows Messenger**. The program will launch and you will be automatically signed in if you are logged on.

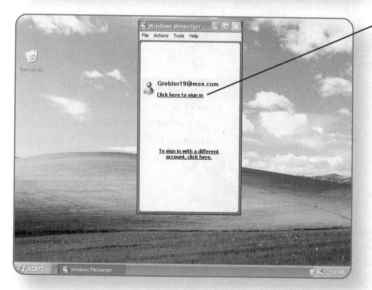

4. **Click here to sign in** if you are not automatically signed on.

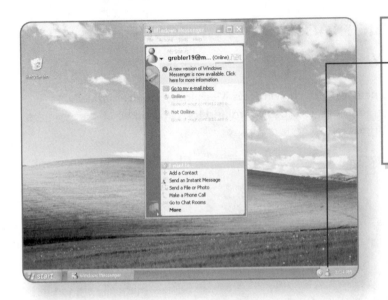

NOTE

An icon will appear in your Notification area whenever you are logged on. This icon will prompt you whenever someone sends you an instant message.

Sending Instant Messages

You can send messages to anyone who has signed up for a Windows Messenger account. Sending a Windows message is similar to e-mailing someone. You simply select a recipient, type in your message, and click send.

1. **Click Actions**. A menu will appear.

2. **Click Send an Instant Message**. This will open a dialog box where you can select a recipient.

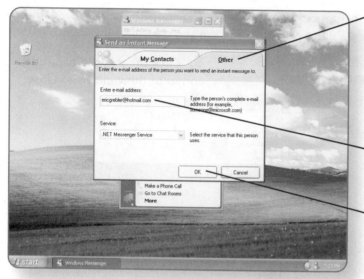

3. Click the **Other** tab. At first, you will have no contacts set up, so to send an instant message, you must go to the Other tab where you can enter the e-mail address of the person you would like to instant message.

4. Type in the **e-mail address** they used to sign up for Windows Messenger.

5. Click OK. Windows Messenger will attempt to contact the recipient. A Conversation window will now open.

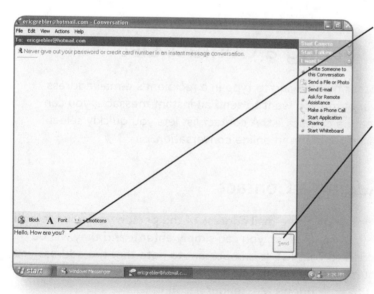

6. Type in your **message.** Once you click Send, everything you type will appear in a window on the computer of the person you are instant messaging.

7. Click Send. The message will be sent.

Every message that is sent back and forth between you and the recipient will appear in the top part of the window.

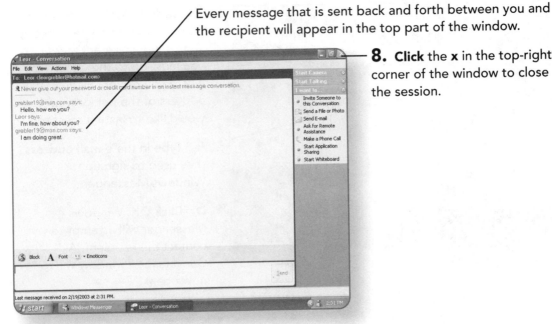

8. **Click** the **x** in the top-right corner of the window to close the session.

Creating a Contact List

Rather than having to type in a recipient's e-mail address every time you want to send an instant message, you can create a contact list. A contact list lets you quickly select participants for an online conversation.

Adding a Contact

If you know the e-mail address of the person you'd like to add to your contact list, you can simply enter it and they will be added to your list. It is important to note that the address you enter must be the same address they used when signing up for their Windows Messenger account.

1. Click Add a Contact.
A dialog box will appear where you can add a contact.

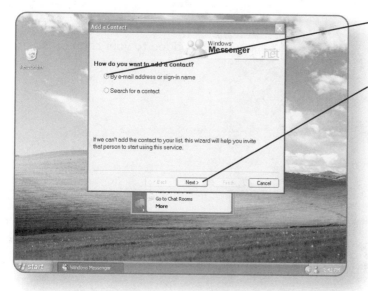

2. Click the **circle** beside By e-mail address or sign-in name, if it is not already selected.

3. Click Next. You will now be able to type in the e-mail address of the person you wish to add to your contact list.

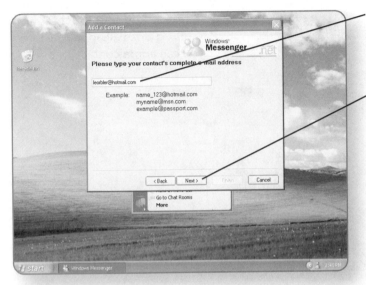

4. **Type their e-mail address**. This is the e-mail address that they used to set up their account.

5. **Click Next** to advance to the next screen of the wizard.

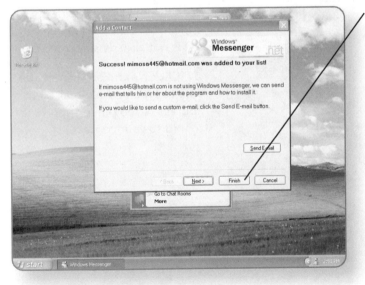

6. **Click Finish**. The person will be added to your contact list.

Receiving Messages

When you are online and someone sends you a message, a little dialog box will automatically appear in the Notification area. If this is the first time that someone has tried to contact you and they are not on your contact list, you'll have to accept them before the Windows message session can begin.

1. **Click** on **any** of the **text** in the dialog box. The Conversation window will open and you can begin the chat session.

Blocking and Unblocking Users

An occasion may arise when you want to prevent someone from sending messages to you. Windows Messenger has a feature that will allow you to block certain people from accessing you if they are using profanity or other behavior that you find offensive, or if you simply don't want them to contact you.

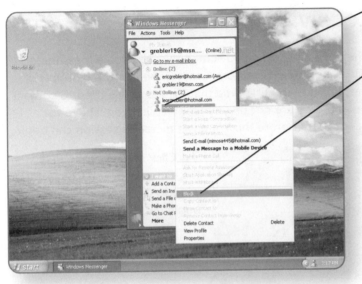

1. **Right-click** on the **user** that you would like to block. A menu will appear.

2. **Click Block**. The user will now be blocked.

The logo beside their name will be enclosed in a circle with a line through it, indicating that they are blocked.

3. **Right-click** on the **user** that you would like to unblock. A menu will appear.

4. **Click Unblock**. The user will now be unblocked.

19

The Address Book

Windows XP Media Center Edition comes with a handy Address
Book that acts as a central location for you to store information on all
of your contacts. You can create separate groups so that you can
logically categorize your contacts. The Address Book also integrates
with Outlook Express. In this chapter, you'll learn how to:

- Add entries to your Address Book
- Manage contacts
- Search for entries
- Import Address Books

The Address Book

The Address Book can be launched from within Outlook Express, or it can be accessed from the Start menu.

1. Click Start. The Start menu will appear.

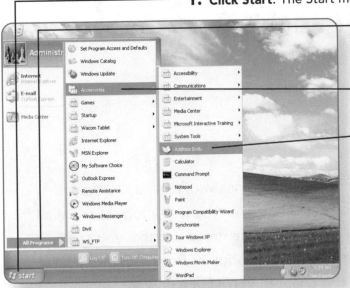

2. Click All Programs. Various programs and categories will appear.

3. Click Accessories. A list of programs will appear.

4. Click Address Book. The Address Book will launch.

Adding Contacts

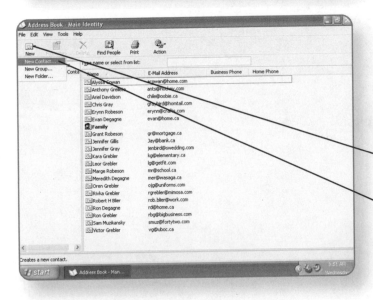

When adding contacts to the Address Book, you can enter as much or as little information about your contact as you choose.

1. Click New. A list of options will appear.

2. Click New Contact. A dialog box will open.

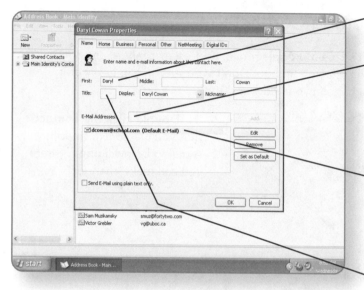

3. Type the **first name** of your contact.

4. Click in the **E-mail Addresses box**. Your cursor will be flashing in the box.

5. Type the **e-mail address** of your contact.

6. Press Enter. The e-mail address will be added. You can repeat Steps 5 and 6 to add multiple e-mail addresses for your contacts.

7. Click in **any other box**. Add as much contact information as you have.

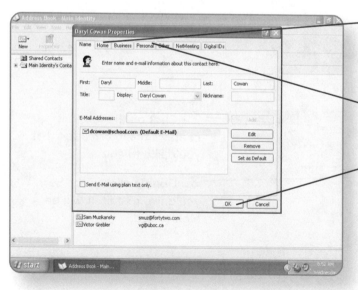

8. Click on the **Home tab**. You can enter as much personal information about your contact as you like on this screen.

9. Click on **any other tab** and enter as much information as you choose.

10. Click OK. The contact will be added to your Address Book.

Editing Contacts

Let's face it. People move, addresses change, and some friends come and go. Don't worry—you can easily edit contacts in your Address Book.

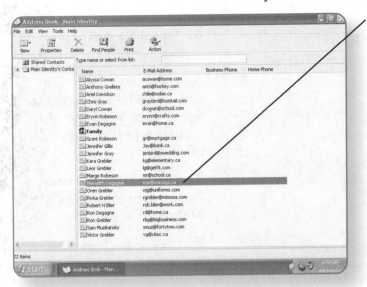

1. Double-click the **contact** that you would like to edit. A dialog box will open, where you can make changes.

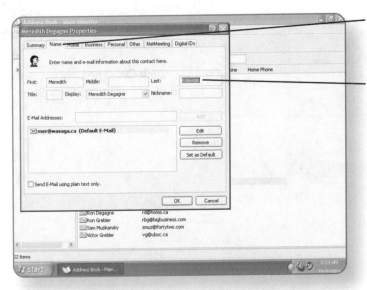

2. Click on the **tab** that contains the information that you'd like to edit.

3. Double-click in the **box** you'd like to edit. It will be highlighted.

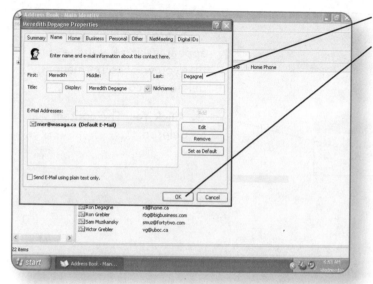

4. **Type** in the **new information**.

5. **Click OK.** The changes will be applied.

Deleting Contacts

Had a falling out with someone? Don't want or need them in your Address Book? Getting rid of them is as easy as pressing a button on your keyboard.

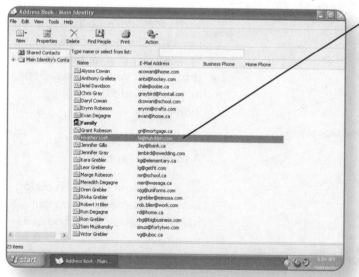

1. **Click** on the **contact** that you would like to delete. It will be highlighted.

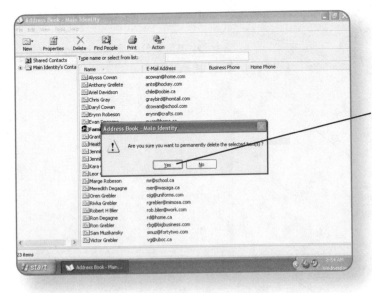

2. **Press** the **Delete** key on the keyboard. A dialog box will appear, asking if you are sure that you want to permanently delete the contact.

3. **Click Yes.** The contact will be deleted.

Creating Groups

If you have some people that you commonly send the same e-mail to, the Address Book allows you to create a group. The advantage of this is that, when you want to send everyone in the group an e-mail, you don't have to type each of their e-mail addresses individually—you can just type the name of the group. You can select members for a group from your Address Book, or you can add them individually.

1. **Click** the **New** button. A menu will appear.

2. **Click New Group.** A dialog box will open where you can name the group and choose its members.

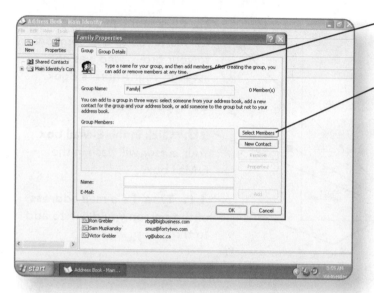

3. **Type** a **name** for your group. You can give the group any name that you want.

4. **Click Select Members**. A dialog box will open, allowing you to choose members for the group from your Address Book.

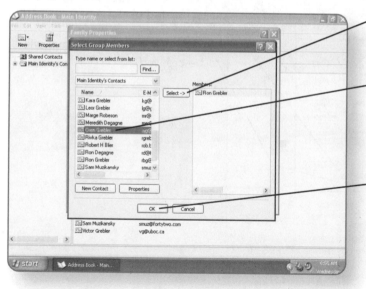

5. **Click** on the **desired member**. The selection will be highlighted.

6. **Click Select**. The member will be added to the group. You can repeat Steps 5 and 6 until you're finished adding people from your Address Book.

7. **Click OK**. You will be returned to the dialog box.

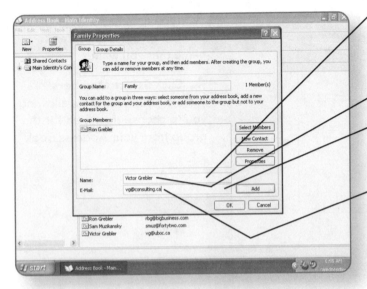

8. **Click** in the **Name box**. This will allow you to add someone to your group who was not listed in your Address Book.

9. **Type** a **name**.

10. **Click** in the **E-Mail box**. Your cursor will flash in the E-Mail box.

11. **Type** the **e-mail address** of the person you'd like to add to the group.

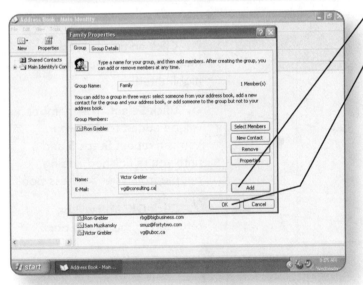

12. **Click Add**. The person will be added to the group.

13. **Click OK**. The group will be created.

Folders

Rather than just having a generic Address Book that contains information on all of your contacts, you can divide the Address Book into logical categories by using folders. Using folders, you can divide your Address Book entries into categories like friends, family, work, or any other category you see fit to create. Folders make managing your Address Book and accessing contact information much easier. Once a folder has been created, you can quickly copy contact entries to it.

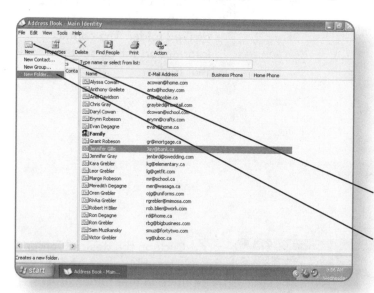

1. Click New. A menu will appear.

2. Click New Folder. A dialog box will open, asking you to name the folder.

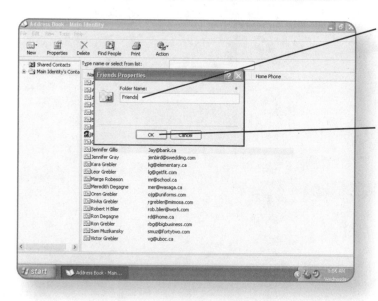

3. Type the **name** of the folder. Try to use a name that will describe the contacts that you will be putting in that folder, like friends or family.

4. Click OK. The folder will be created.

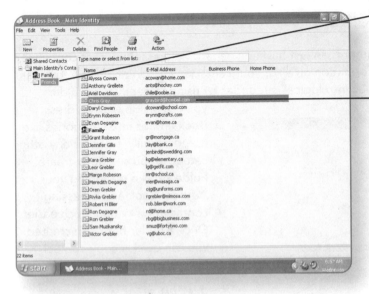

5. **Click** on **Main Identity's Contacts**. A list of all of your contacts will appear in the right pane of the window.

6. **Click** and **drag** a **contact** from the window onto the desired folder. The contact information will be sent to that folder.

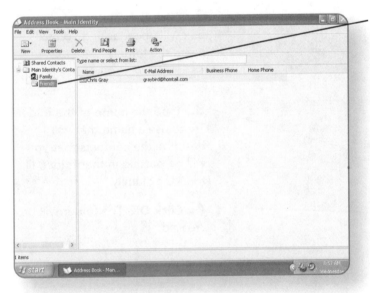

7. **Click** on the **desired folder**. You'll be able to see who is included in that folder, as its contents will appear in the right pane of the window.

Finding Contacts

If you are looking for a specific contact, you can easily find it using the Address Book's built-in search engine.

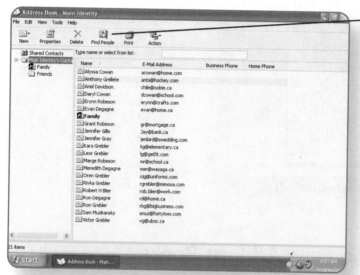

1. Click the **Find People** button. A dialog box will appear, where you can enter any information that you have on the contact you are looking for.

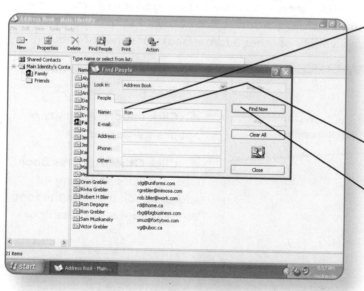

2. Click in the **box** that contains the search criteria that you know. For example, if you're searching for a contact and you only know that person's name, click in the Name box.

3. Type the **criteria** that you know about the contact.

4. Click Find Now. The search will be conducted, and any contact matching the criteria that you entered will be displayed in the bottom part of the window.

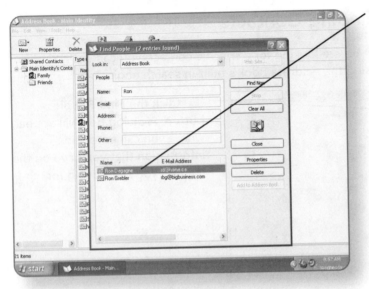

5. Double-click on the **desired contact** to view all of their information.

Importing Address Books

If you have already created an address book in another application, there's no sense in having to re-create everything from scratch. The Address Book allows you to import entries from a variety of other address books or spreadsheets.

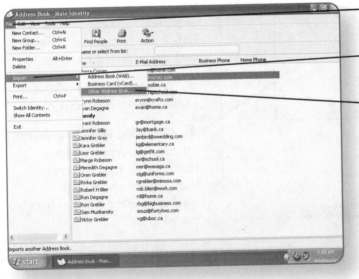

1. Click File. The File menu will appear.

2. Click Import. A variety of options will appear.

3. Click Other Address Book, unless you are importing an address book that is in the form WAB (Windows Address Book).

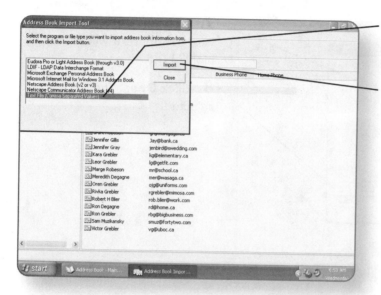

4. Click the **type** of address you wish to import. It will be highlighted.

5. Click Import. You will now be asked to select the file.

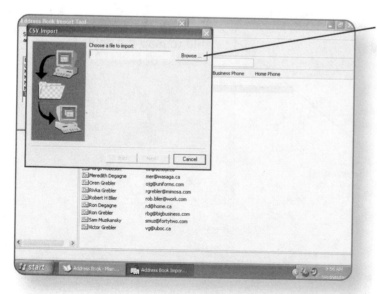

6. Click Browse. A dialog box will open, allowing you to select a file.

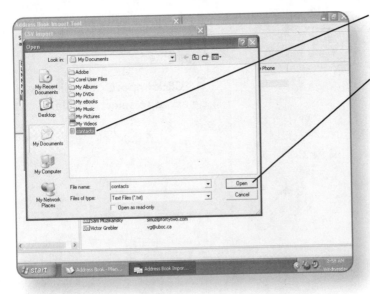

7. **Click** on the **file** that you wish to import. It will be highlighted.

8. **Click Open**. The file will be selected.

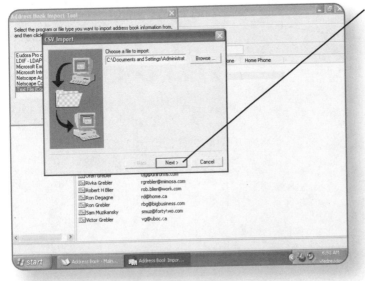

9. **Click Next**. You will now be able to map the fields to your Address Book.

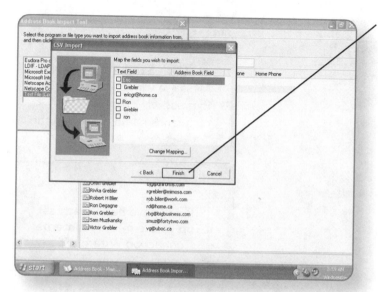

10. **Click Finish**. The contacts will be imported to your Address Book.

E-Mailing from Your Address Book

Even though the Address Book can be accessed from inside Outlook Express, the opposite is also true. You can pick a recipient and then launch Outlook Express from within the Address Book.

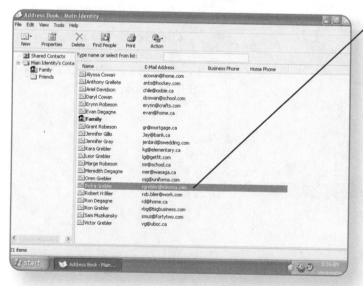

1. **Click** the **recipient** that you'd like to e-mail. They will be highlighted.

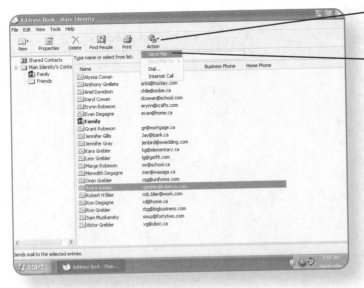

2. **Click Action**. A menu of options will appear.

3. **Click Send Mail**. The New Message window of Outlook Express will open with the recipient's name already in the To: section.

NOTE

If you have not already set up your e-mail, the Internet Connection Wizard will appear, and you will be prompted to provide information so that your e-mail account can be set up.

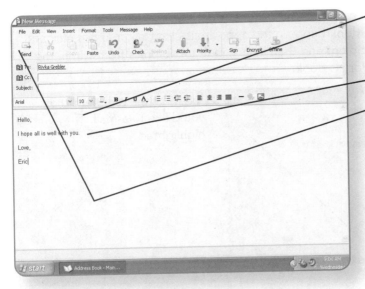

4. **Click** in the **message** body. Your cursor will be flashing in that section.

5. **Type** in the **message**.

6. **Click Send**. The message will be sent, the window will close, and you will return to the Address Book.

20

Printers and Printing

With the invention of electronic mail, e-books, online catalogs, and—of course—the Web, you might figure that the need for printing and printers would start to decline. If you thought that, you'd be wrong. The primary output for documents, Web pages, and e-mails is still the printer. The good news is that Windows XP Media Center Edition allows you to quickly set up, install, and configure your printer. In this chapter, you'll learn how to:

- Install a printer
- Set a default printer
- Configure a printer
- Print a document
- Fax a document

Installing a Local Printer

One of the greatest features of Windows XP Media Center Edition is that almost every piece of hardware that you plug into the computer will automatically be recognized and configured using what's called "Plug and Play" technology. If your printer connects via a USB cable, there's a good likelihood that it will be automatically recognized. There may be varieties of printers that Windows XP Media Center Edition will not automatically recognize; if that's the case for you, you will have to manually install the printer. Before you begin, make sure that the printer is plugged into the computer and powered on.

1. Click Start. The Start menu will appear.

2. Click Control Panel. This will open the Control Panel window.

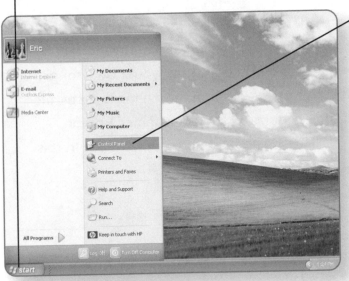

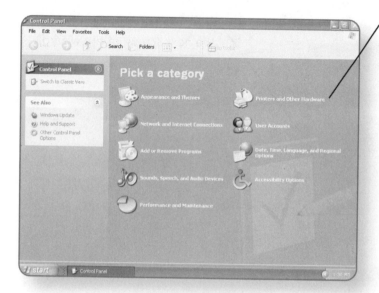

3. **Click Printers and Other Hardware**. This will open a window where you can add a printer.

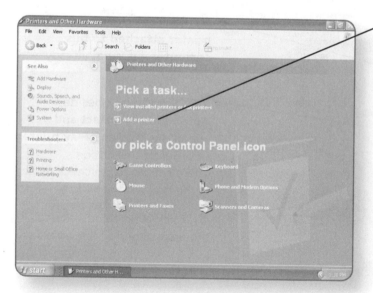

4. **Click Add a printer**. The Add Printer Wizard will now run.

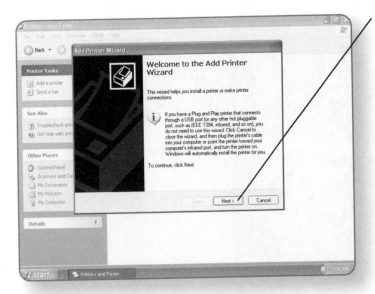

5. **Click Next** to advance to the next screen of the wizard.

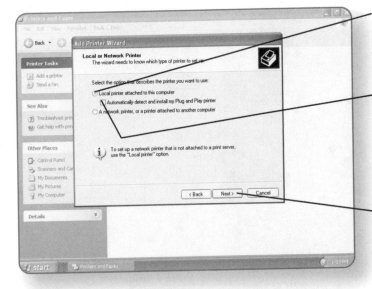

6. **Click** the **circle** beside **Local printer attached to this computer** if it is not already selected.

7. **Click** the **box** beside **Automatically detect and install my Plug and Play printer** to deselect this option. There should be no check mark in the box.

8. **Click Next** to advance to the next screen of the wizard.

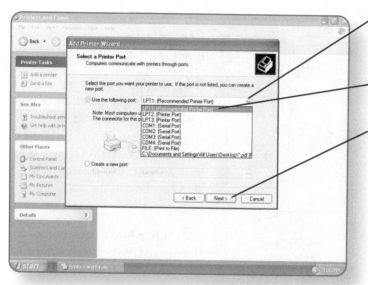

9. **Click** on the **down arrow** beside **Use the following port**. A list of ports will be displayed.

10. **Click** the **desired port**. It will now be selected.

11. **Click Next** to advance to the next screen of the wizard.

12. **Click** the **manufacturer** of your computer in the left part of the window. You can scroll through the different manufacturers by using the up and down arrows.

13. **Click** your **printer** from the right part of the window.

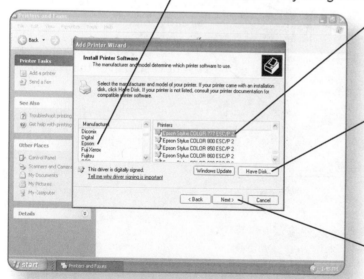

NOTE

If the manufacturer of your printer is not listed, and you have the disks that came with your printer, press the Have Disk button and follow the instructions.

14. **Click Next** to advance to the next screen of the wizard.

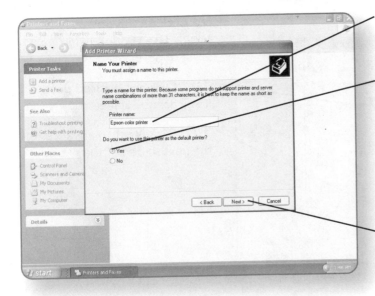

15. **Type** a **name** for your printer. Make sure that the name is not more than 31 characters.

16. **Click** the **circle** beside **Yes** or **No** to decide whether or not you want to make this printer the default printer. This simply means that when you go to print a document, this printer will show up first in the list, if you have more than one printer.

17. **Click Next** to advance to the next screen of the Wizard.

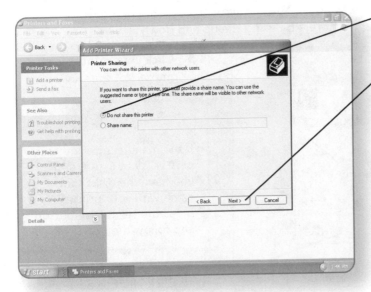

18. **Click** the **circle** beside **Do not share this printer** if it is not already selected.

19. **Click Next** to advance to the next screen of the wizard.

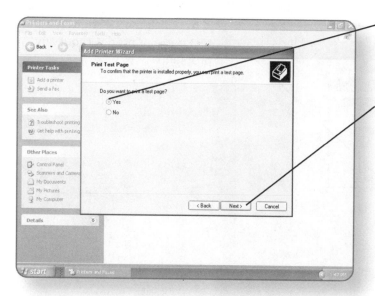

20. **Click** the **circle** beside **Yes** if it is not already selected. This will print a test page to ensure your printer is working properly.

21. **Click Next** to advance to the next screen of the wizard.

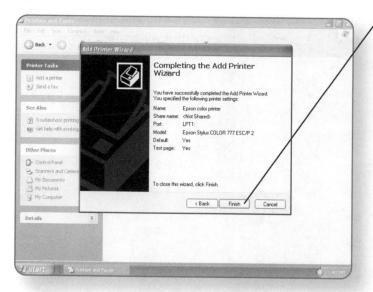

22. **Click** the **Finish** button if everything seems correct in the summary. A test page will now be printed.

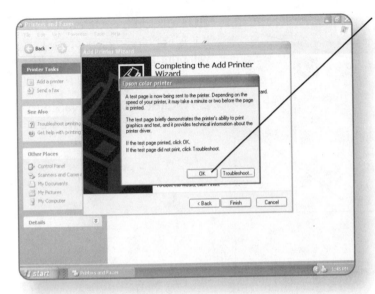

23. **Click** the **OK** button if the test page printed without any problems.

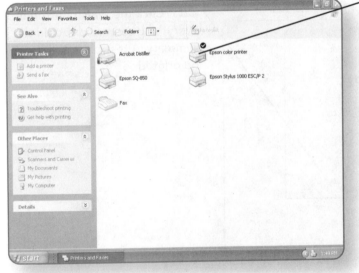

An icon for the printer that you created will appear in the Printers and Faxes window.

Changing the Default Printer

If you have more than one printer, you may want to change which printer is the default. The default printer should be the one that you use the most often, as it will show up first in the Printers list whenever you print from an application. The point of having a default printer is that it will save you time, as you won't have to pick a printer when printing—the default will automatically be selected.

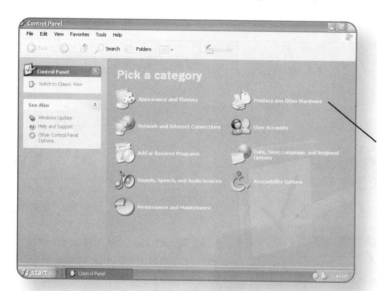

1. Click Printers and Other Hardware. This will open a window where you can choose a task.

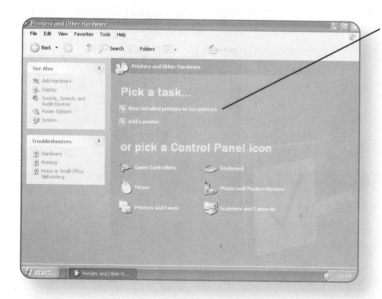

2. Click View installed printers or fax printers. A list of all of your installed printers will appear.

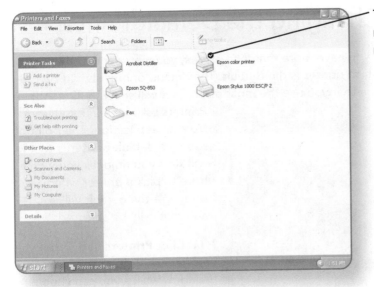

The current default printer is represented by a white check mark in a black circle.

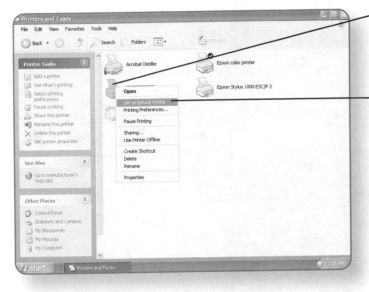

3. **Right-click** on the **icon** of the printer that you would like to set as your default. A menu will appear.

4. **Click Set as Default Printer**. This printer will now be set up as your default printer.

Printing a Document

Almost every program that you install in Windows XP Media Center Edition will have a Print function that works in a similar fashion. In most cases, the Print command will appear under the File menu. In this example, we will use Internet Explorer to print a Web page, but you can use almost any other program.

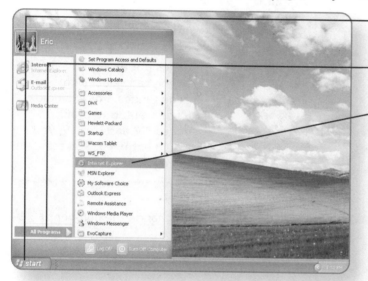

1. Click Start. The Start menu will appear.

2. Click All Programs. A list of programs will appear.

3. Click Internet Explorer. Internet Explorer will now be launched.

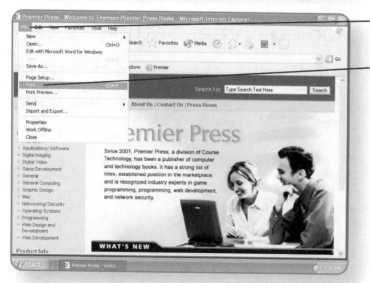

4. Click File. The File menu will appear.

5. Click Print. The Print dialog box will now open.

TIP

Pressing Ctrl+P, in most applications, will launch the Print dialog box.

6. Click the **desired printer**. If you want to print to your default printer, you can skip this step, as it will already be selected.

7. Click the **desired Page Range**. If your document is more than one page, you do not have to print every page.

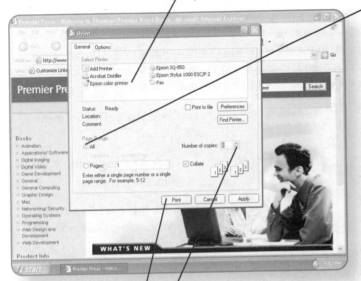

TIP

You can select a range of pages (for example, 3-5), or you can select single-page ranges. For example, if you wanted to print pages 4-7 and page 9, you would enter 4-7, 9 in the Pages box.

8. Click the **up** or **down arrow** to change the number of copies you'd like.

9. Click Print. The document will be printed.

Changing Printer Settings

You may want to change some of the settings for your printer. This is especially the case if you'll be printing out your digital photos, as you'll want to set the type of paper used, the size of the paper, and the layout.

1. **Click** the **Start** button. The Start menu will appear.

2. **Click Control Panel.** The Control Panel window will open.

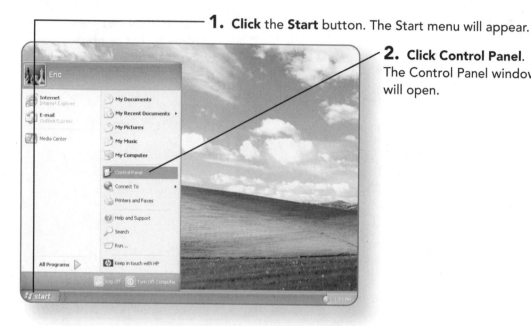

3. **Click Printers and Other Hardware.** This will open a window where you can choose a task.

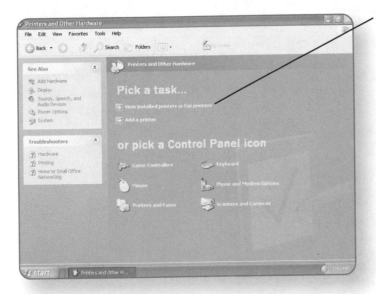

4. Click View installed printers or fax printers. A list of installed printers will appear.

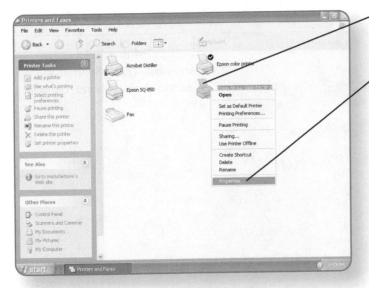

5. Right-click on the **Printer** that you would like to configure. A menu will appear.

6. Click Properties. This will open up the Printer Properties dialog box.

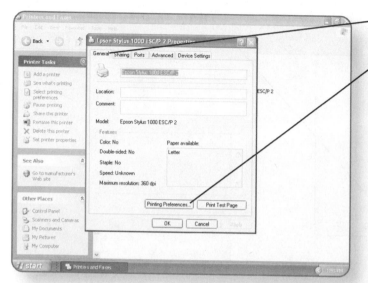

7. Click the **General tab** if it is not already selected.

8. Click Printing Preferences. This will open up the Preferences dialog box for your particular printer. Every printer will have different printer options, so yours might not look identical to what you see here.

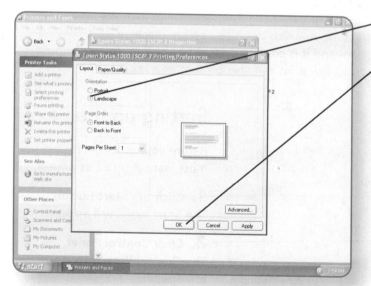

9. Make any **desired changes** to the printer preferences.

10. Click OK to accept the changes that you've made.

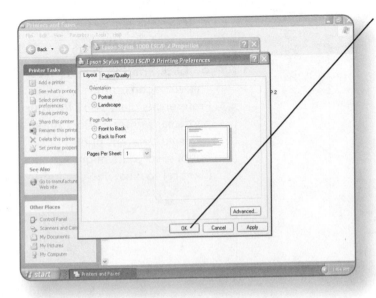

11. Click OK to close the Properties dialog box. The changes will now take effect.

Faxing

Your computer also doubles as a fax machine if you have a modem and it is connected to a phone line. Any document that you can print can also be sent as a fax.

Setting up the Fax

Before you can begin faxing, you must first set up a Fax printer.

1. Click the **Start** button. The Start menu will appear.

2. Click Control Panel. The Control Panel window will open.

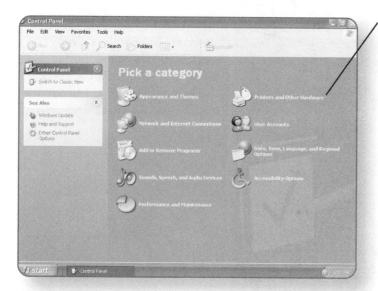

3. Click Printers and Other Hardware. This will open a window where you can choose a task.

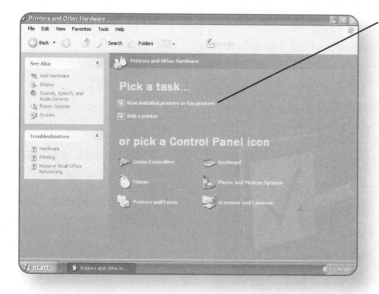

4. Click View installed printers or fax printers. A list of installed printers will appear.

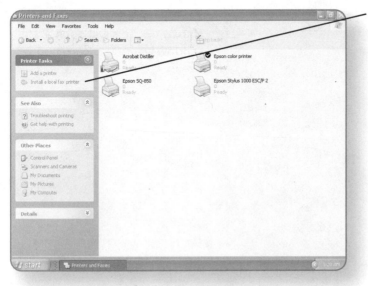

5. **Click Install a local fax printer**. The computer will automatically install the fax machine. When it is complete, an icon representing the fax machine will appear.

Faxing a Document

You can fax a document just as you would print it; the only difference is that you select the fax machine as your printer. Before a document can be faxed, you must make sure that your telephone line is connected to your computer.

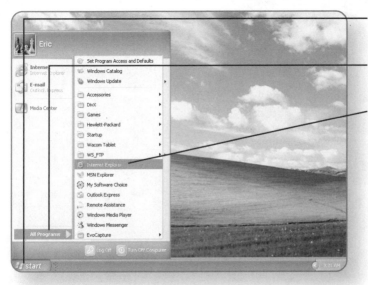

1. **Click Start**. The Start menu will appear.

2. **Click All Programs**. A list of programs will appear.

3. **Click Internet Explorer**. Internet Explorer will now be launched.

4. Click File. The File menu will appear.

5. Click Print. The Print dialog box will now open.

NOTE

We are using Internet Explorer to fax a document, but you can fax from any application that allows you to print.

6. Click Fax as the printer. It will be highlighted, once selected.

7. Click Print. The Fax Configuration Wizard will appear if it is the first time you are trying to send a fax.

8. **Click Next** to advance to the next screen of the wizard.

9. **Type** any personal **information** that you'd like to include in the cover page.

10. **Click Next** to advance to the next screen of the wizard.

11. Click Finish. The wizard will close and the Send Fax Wizard will start.

12. Click Next to start the wizard.

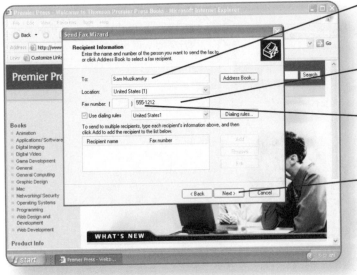

13. Type the **name** of the person you are sending the fax to.

14. Press the **Tab** key to advance to the Fax number box.

15. Type the **fax number** of the person you are sending the fax to.

16. Click **Next** to advance to the next screen.

17. Click the **box** beside **Select a cover page template with the following information** if you want to add a cover page to your fax.

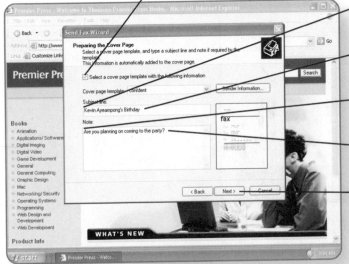

18. Click in the **Subject line** box.

19. Type the **subject** for your fax.

20. Press the **Tab** key. You will advance to the Note section.

21. Type in any **notes** for your cover page.

22. Click **Next** to advance to the next screen of the wizard.

23. **Click** on the **desired option** for scheduling the send of the fax. A dot will appear beside the selection you've chosen.

24. **Click Next** to advance to the next screen of the wizard.

25. **Click Finish**. The fax will be sent.

The Fax Monitor dialog box will open and attempt to send your fax.

Printing Controls

If you are printing many documents, or if you have multiple users accessing certain printers, being able to control the print jobs becomes important. While there are print jobs waiting, you can monitor their progress, pause the printing, or delete the print job altogether.

Monitoring Printing

To monitor printing, there must be at least one print job sent to the printer. If it hasn't been completely printed, you can monitor its progress. You'll be able to see the status of the print job, its size, how many pages it is, and when it was submitted for printing.

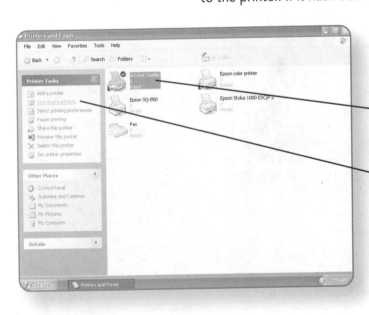

1. **Click** the **printer** that you'd like to monitor. It will be highlighted, once selected.

2. **Click See what's printing** in the Printer Tasks area. A dialog box will now open showing you the status of your print jobs.

Pausing a Print Job

If you want to pause a particular print job in order to let other printing take priority, you can do so while monitoring the print jobs.

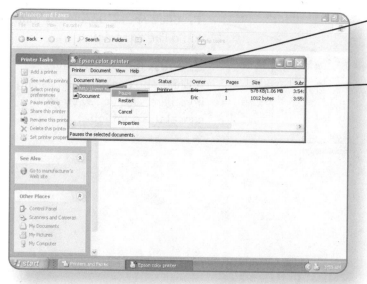

1. Right-click on the **document** that you'd like to pause. A menu will appear.

2. Click Pause. The print job will be paused. It can then be restarted, once you'd like it to print.

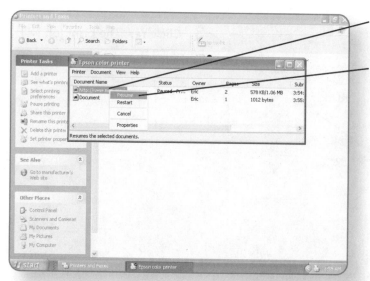

3. Right-click on the **document**. A menu will appear.

4. Click Resume. The print job will now be resumed.

Deleting a Print Job

If you want to remove a print job from the queue altogether, it can be deleted. Keep in mind that you are only deleting the print job, not the document itself.

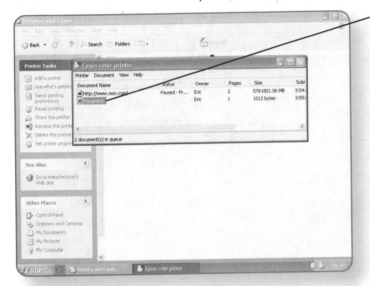

1. **Click** on the **document** that you'd like to remove.

2. **Press** the **Delete** key. A dialog box will appear, asking if you are sure you want to cancel the print job.

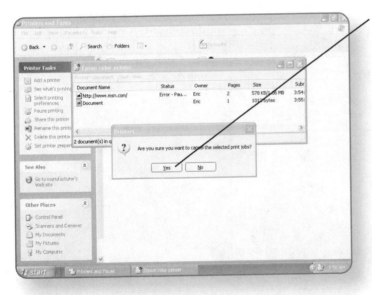

3. **Click Yes**. The print job will be canceled.

21

Accessibility

Understanding the fact that not everyone uses a computer in the same way and that some people are differently abled, Windows XP Media Center Edition provides a variety of Accessibility features. In this chapter, you'll learn how to:

- Run the Accessibility Wizard
- Use the Magnifier
- Run the Narrator
- Use the On-Screen Keyboard

The Accessibility Wizard

If you have a physical limitation, it may be a good idea to first run the Accessibility Wizard. This wizard will ask you questions regarding your physical limitations and will adjust the settings of your computer accordingly. Windows XP Media Center Edition will make adjustments based on visual, hearing, and mobility limitations. Depending on what selections you make while going through the Accessibility Wizard, some of the following steps may be bypassed.

1. **Click Start**. The Start menu will appear.

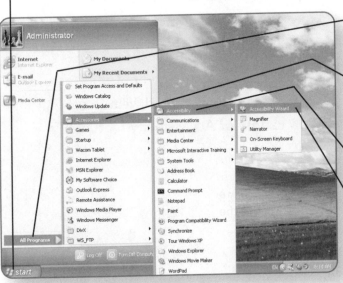

2. **Click All Programs**. A list of programs and categories will appear.

3. **Click Accessories**. The programs that fall under the Accessories category will appear.

4. **Click Accessibility**. Various accessibility options will appear.

5. **Click Accessibility Wizard**. The Accessibility Wizard will launch.

6. Click Next to start the wizard. The wizard will ask you a variety of questions with regards to your accessibility needs. Continue going through the wizard until it has completed.

The Magnifier

The Magnifier allows you to zoom in to areas of your screen if you have a visual impairment. When you hover your mouse pointer over a certain area, that area will be magnified in a window that is across the top of your screen.

1. **Click Start**. The Start menu will appear.

2. **Click All Programs**. A list of programs and categories will appear.

3. **Click Accessories**. The programs that fall under the Accessories category will appear.

4. **Click Accessibility**. Various accessibility options will appear.

5. **Click Magnifier**. The Magnifier will launch and a dialog box will appear.

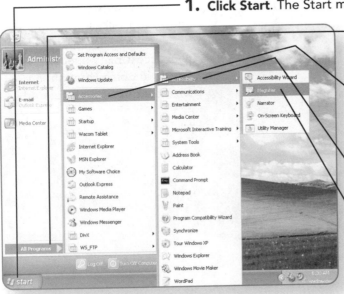

A magnification area will appear on the top part of the screen after the Magnifier has been launched.

6. **Click OK**. This will close the dialog box.

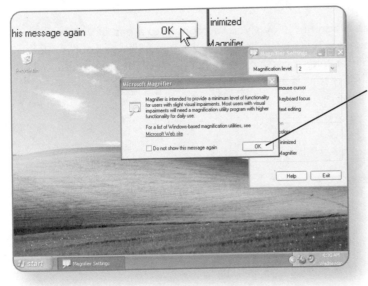

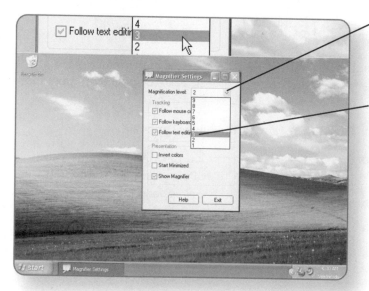

7. **Click** the **down arrow** beside Magnification level. A list of different magnification levels will appear.

8. **Click** the **desired level**. It will be highlighted.

9. **Position** the **mouse pointer** over any part of the screen. It will be magnified in the top part of the window.

10. **Click Exit** when you are finished using the Magnifier.

The Narrator

Another feature for those with visual impairments is the Narrator. The Narrator is a basic text-to-speech program that will read elements of the screen.

1. **Click Start**. The Start menu will appear.

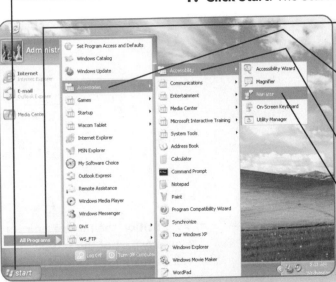

2. **Click All Programs**. A list of programs and categories will appear.

3. **Click Accessories**. The programs that fall under the Accessories category will appear.

4. **Click Accessibility**. Various accessibility options will appear.

5. **Click Narrator**. The Narrator will launch and a dialog box will appear.

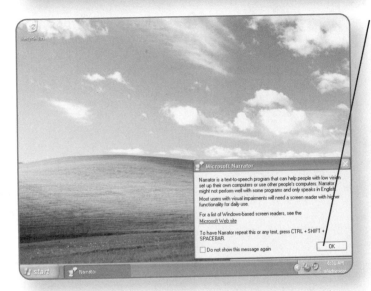

6. **Click OK** to close the dialog box that explains what the Narrator does. The Narrator will now dictate any action that you take with the mouse, and it will read any parts of the screen.

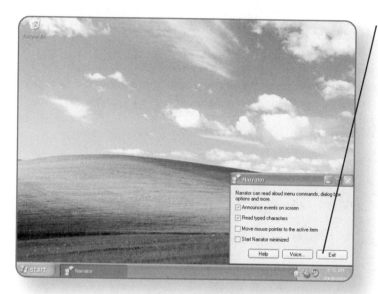

7. **Click Exit** when finished with the Narrator.

8. **Click Yes** to confirm that you want to exit the Narrator.

TIP

Press Ctrl+Shift+Spacebar to have the Narrator repeat any text.

On-Screen Keyboard

If you have difficulty using a regular keyboard, you can take advantage of the On-Screen Keyboard. It allows you to apply keystrokes by clicking on a visual image of a keyboard.

1. Click Start. The Start menu will appear.

2. Click All Programs. A list of programs and categories will appear.

3. Click Accessories. The programs that fall under the Accessories category will appear.

4. Click Accessibility. Various accessibility options will appear.

5. Click On-Screen Keyboard. The On-Screen Keyboard will launch.

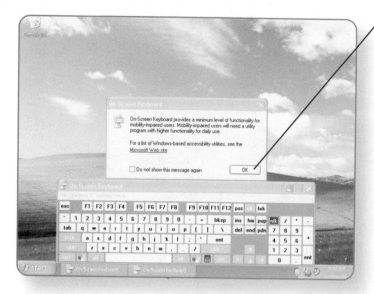

6. Click OK to close the dialog box that describes the On-Screen Keyboard.

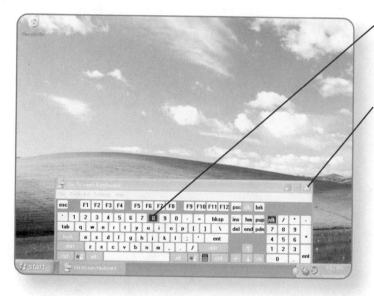

7. Click on **any key** on the On-Screen Keyboard. It will have the same effect as if you were pressing on a regular keyboard.

8. Click the **x** in the top-right corner of the On-Screen Keyboard to close it when you are finished.

22

The Control Panel

The Control Panel is the nerve center for all of the functions for your computer. From the Control Panel, you can adjust most of the basic settings of your computer. Whether it's adding programs, installing fonts, or changing your display, the Control Panel is your one-stop access for changing the configuration of your computer. In this chapter, you'll learn how to:

- Access the Control Panel
- Adjust system settings
- Control users
- Back up data

Accessing the Control Panel

The Control Panel allows you to adjust almost all system settings. Because of its importance, it can be accessed directly from the Start menu.

1. **Click Start**. The Start menu will appear.

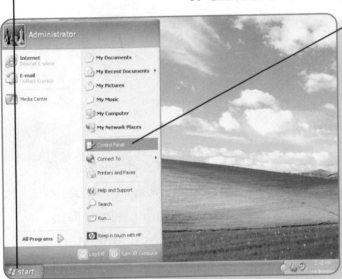

2. **Click Control Panel**. The Control Panel window will open.

Users

Have you ever let someone else use your car? If you're anything like me, it frustrates you when other people mess with the position of your seat, change your radio presets, or adjust your mirrors. You don't have to worry about people messing up your settings with Windows XP Media Center Edition. When your computer was first set up, at least one user was created. If you have more than one person accessing the computer, it's a good idea to set up individual accounts. By having separate accounts, each person who accesses the computer can control individual preferences.

Adding a User

The Control Panel gives you access to the user accounts on your computer.

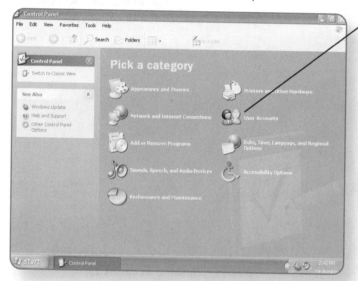

1. Click User Accounts.
The User Accounts window will open.

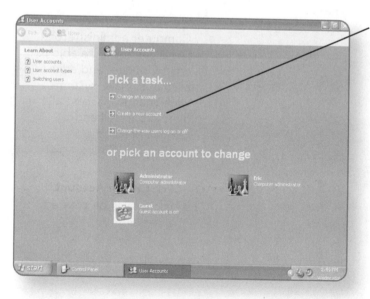

2. Click Create a new account.
You will now be able to name the account.

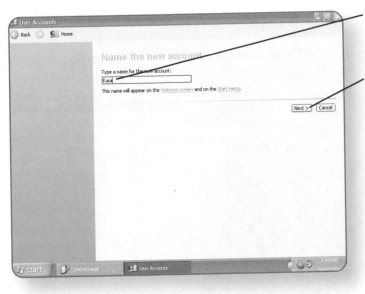

3. **Type** a **name** for the account. Typically, you would use the first name of the user.

4. **Click Next**. You can now choose the account type.

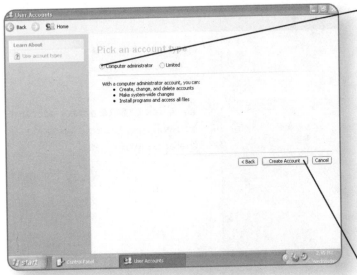

5. **Click** the **circle** beside the **desired account type**.

NOTE

If you set up an account as Computer administrator, the account will be able to create, delete, and adjust accounts; make system-wide changes; access all files; and install and remove programs.

6. **Click Create Account**. The account will be created.

Adjusting User Settings

Windows XP Media Center Edition allows you to customize all of the settings for users. Included in the options is the ability to change the name of a user, create a password, change the photo associated with the user, change the type of account, or delete an account.

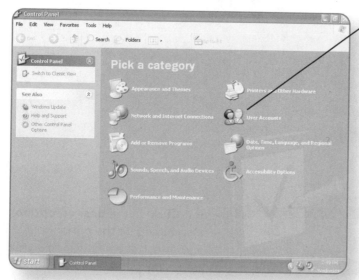

1. Click User Accounts.
The User Accounts window will open.

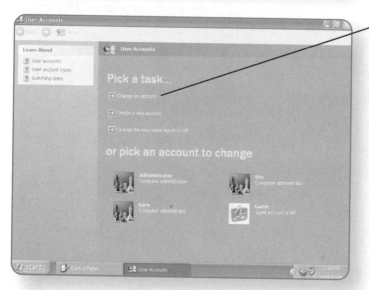

2. Click Change an account.
You will now be asked to pick the account that you would like to change.

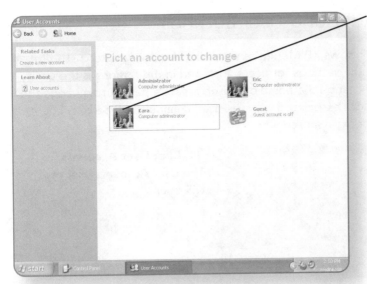

3. **Click** on the **account** that you would like to change. A list of options will now appear.

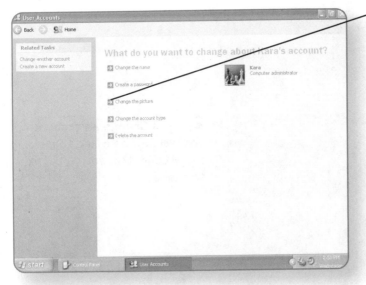

4. **Click** on the **desired option**. Depending on the option that you select, the next window you select will differ. Simply follow the instructions that are presented to you on the screen.

Installing Fonts

Your Windows XP Media Center Edition computer comes with a variety of different fonts for you to choose from when formatting text. You can also add any other fonts to your machine through the Control Panel. Typically, additional fonts can be found included with certain software packages, downloaded from the Internet, or purchased from a software vendor.

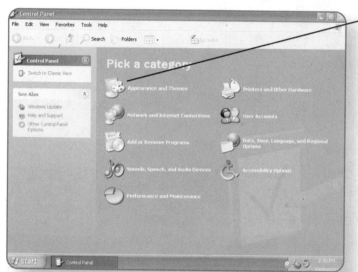

1. Click Appearance and Themes. The window will change to give you appearance and theme options.

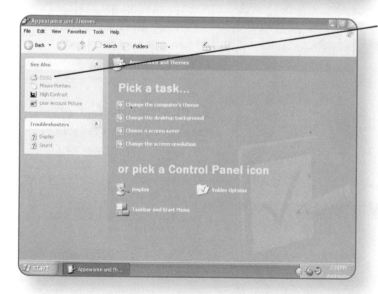

2. Click Fonts in the See Also section. A window with all of your fonts will appear.

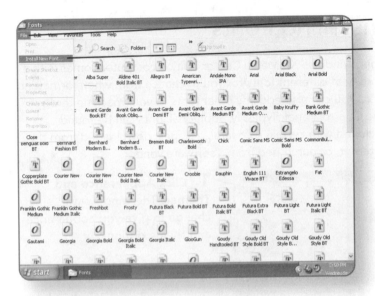

3. **Click File**. A menu will appear.

4. **Click Install New Font.** A dialog box will appear.

5. **Click** on the **location** of the font or fonts that you want to install.

6. **Click** the **font** that you want to install.

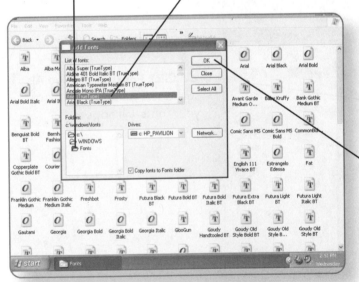

TIP

You can hold down the Ctrl key and click on more than one font to select multiple fonts.

7. **Click OK**. The font will install and will be available in any application where you can access fonts.

8. Click the **x** in the top-right corner to close the Fonts window, once you are finished.

Adjusting the System Sound

Although most programs that have the ability to play music or sounds have their own volume settings, you can control the master volume level for the entire computer.

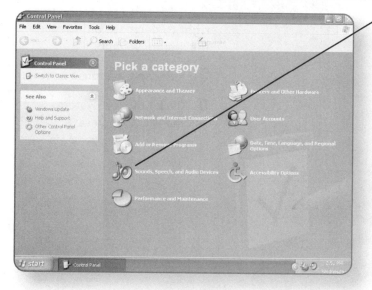

1. Click Sounds, Speech, and Audio Devices. The window will now change to offer you options for the system sounds.

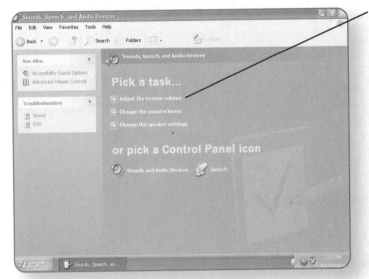

2. Click Adjust the system volume. A dialog box will appear where you can adjust the system volume.

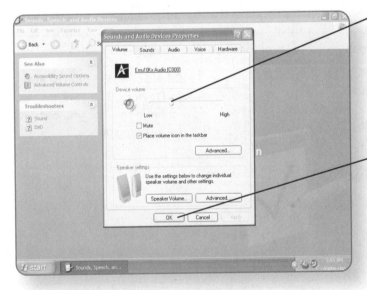

3. Position the **mouse pointer over the slider bar**.

4. Click and **drag** to the **left** or **right** to decrease or increase the system volume.

5. Release the **mouse button**.

6. Click OK. The system volume will now be set.

Adding Programs

Most programs that you purchase can be installed just by inserting the CD into the drive and following the on-screen instructions. You can, however, use the Control Panel to install a program so that the computer can keep track of the programs on your machine.

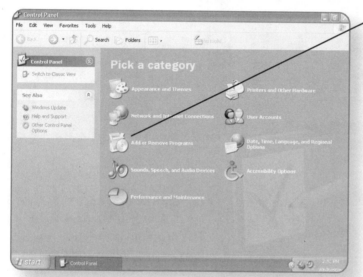

1. Click **Add or Remove Programs**. A dialog box will open where you can install or remove programs.

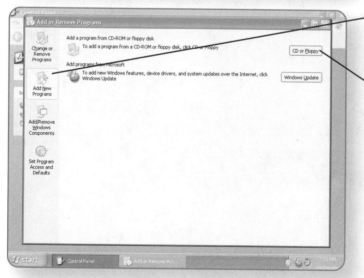

2. Click **Add New Programs**. You will have two choices offered to you.

3. Click **CD or Floppy**. A wizard will now run, taking you through the installation process.

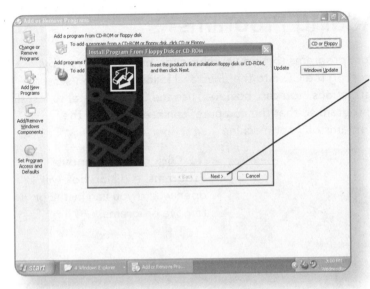

4. **Insert** the **CD or floppy** of the program you want to install into the appropriate drive.

5. **Click Next**. Windows XP Media Center Edition will now search your drives for the installation disk or CD.

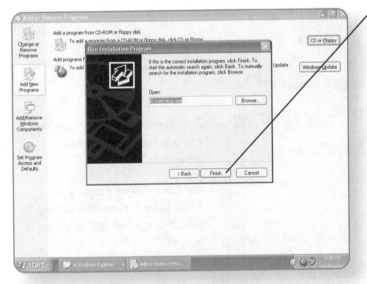

6. **Click Finish**, once the installation file has been found. The program installation will now begin. Follow the on-screen instructions for installing the program.

Removing Programs

If you install a program using the Control Panel, it will be much easier to remove it if you decide that you no longer want it on your computer. Even if you didn't use the Control Panel to install the program, the proper way to remove it is to attempt to find it in the program list of the Control Panel and then uninstall it.

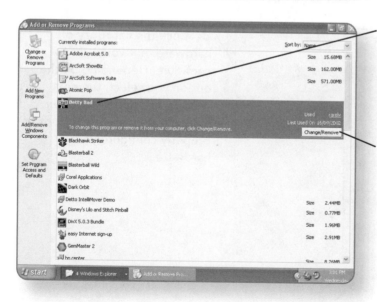

1. Click Add or Remove Programs. A dialog box will open where you can install or remove programs.

2. Click on the **program** that you want to uninstall. If the program is not listed, you will have to use the program's uninstall feature, rather than using the Control Panel.

3. Click Change/Remove. The uninstall process will begin.

Configuring Hardware

Windows XP Media Center Edition does an excellent job of recognizing hardware that you attach to your computer and configuring it. Typically, when you purchase new hardware, it will come with device drivers on CD or disk that will guide you through the installation process. Your best bet is to first use these disks to install the hardware and then take advantage of the Control Panel to further configure.

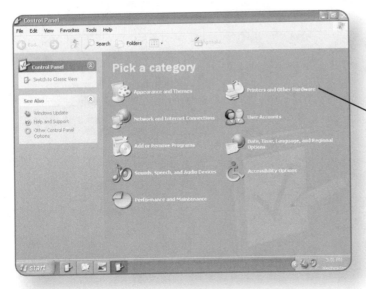

1. Click Printers and Other Hardware. A window will appear with various hardware options.

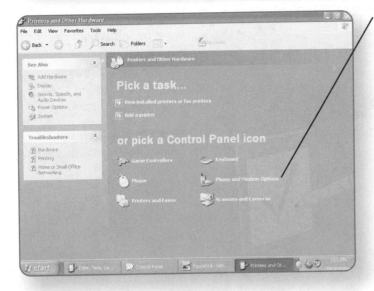

2. Click the **category** of hardware that you want to configure. Depending on the option you select, the next window to appear will differ. Follow the on-screen options to properly configure your hardware.

Adjusting the Date and Time

The Control Panel allows you to quickly configure the time and date settings of your computer. Once they are set up, Windows XP Media Center Edition will automatically change the time when the time changes at different points during the year.

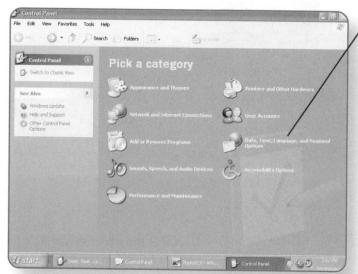

1. Click Date, Time, Language, and Regional Options. The screen will change, giving you a variety of options.

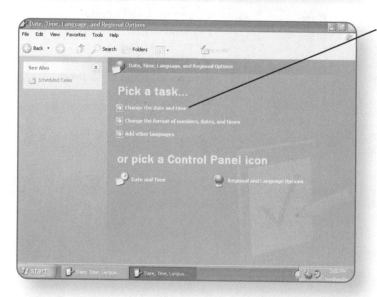

2. Click Change the date and time. A dialog box will appear allowing you to change the date and time.

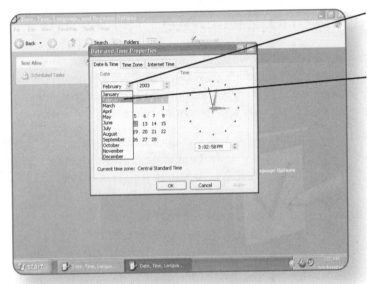

3. Click the **down arrow** beside the month. A list of all of the months of the year will appear.

4. Click the **current month**. It will be selected.

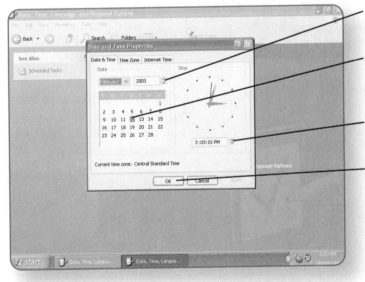

5. Click the **up** or **down arrows** to adjust the year.

6. Click on the **date** in the calendar. It will appear highlighted.

7. Click the **up** or **down arrows** to adjust the time.

8. Click OK. The time will be set.

Backing Up Data

We store a lot of valuable information on our computers, much of which we couldn't afford to do without. Because computers are made up of so many different parts, there is always the potential that something may malfunction and your data will be lost. For that reason, it's always a good idea to back up your data. Windows XP Media Center Edition makes it easy to back up your data by providing a wizard that will step you through the process.

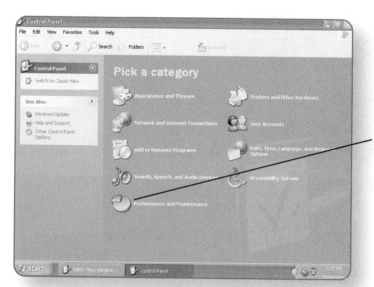

1. Click Performance and Maintenance. The screen will change to give you a variety of maintenance functions.

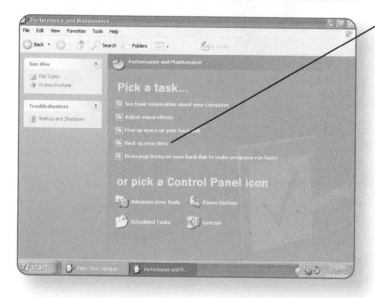

2. Click Back up your data. The Backup or Restore Wizard will open.

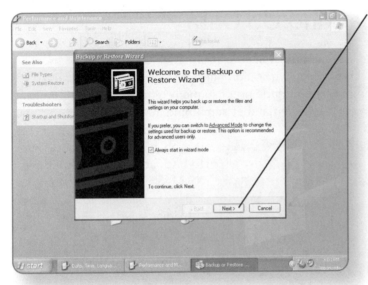

3. **Click Next** to start the wizard.

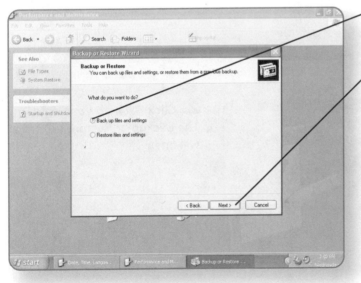

4. **Click** the **circle** beside **Back up files and settings** if it is not already selected.

5. **Click Next** to advance to the screen where you select what files you'd like to back up.

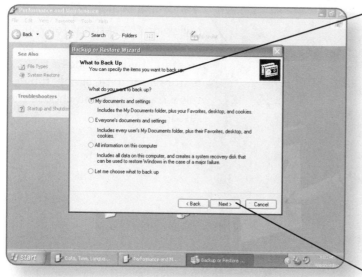

6. **Click** the **circle** beside the **desired option**. A dot will appear inside the circle of the option you selected.

NOTE

If you select the Let me choose what to back up option, another screen will appear where you can select which files and folders you'd like to back up.

7. **Click Next**. You will now choose where you want to create the backup file.

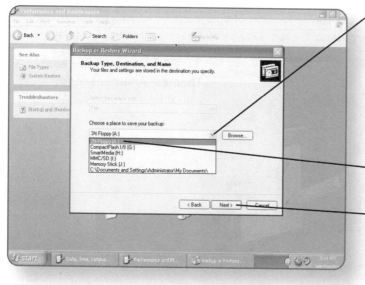

8. **Click** the **down arrow** below **Choose a place to save your backup**. A list of storage devices will appear. Alternatively, you can click the Browse button and select a location on your computer or network to create the backup.

9. **Click** the **desired location.** It will be selected.

10. **Click Next**. You will now be able to finalize the backup.

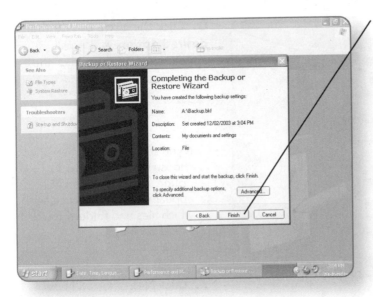

11. **Click Finish** after reviewing the settings for your backup. The backup file will be created. If you ever need to restore your data, simply run this wizard again and choose the restore option.

Displays

Windows XP Media Center Edition allows you to quickly change the settings for the display you are using. You can change the resolution of your display, as well as the quality of the colors. It even allows you to set up multiple displays.

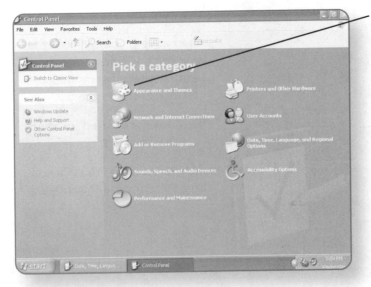

1. **Click Appearance and Themes**. Another window will open.

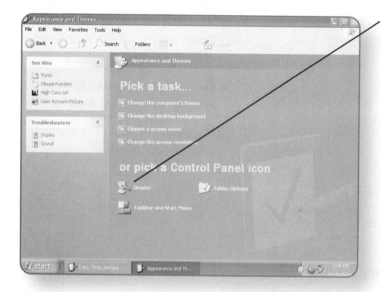

2. Click Display. The Display dialog box will open.

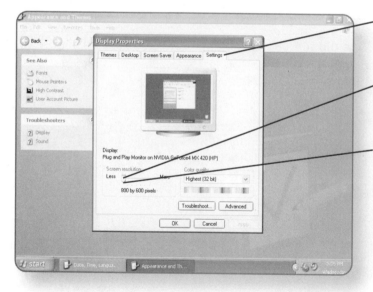

3. Click the **Settings** tab. You will now be able to modify the monitor settings.

4. Position your **cursor** over the **slider bar** under Screen resolution.

5. Click and **drag** to the **left** or **right** to adjust the resolution.

6. Release the **mouse button**. A preview of the resolution will appear in the picture of the monitor.

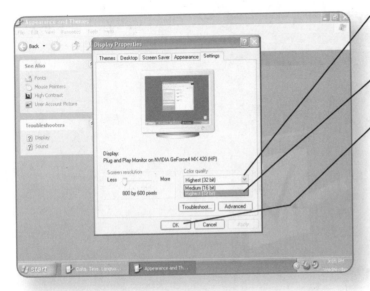

7. **Click** the **down arrow** under **Color quality**. A list of options will appear.

8. **Click** the **desired quality level**. It will now be highlighted.

9. **Click OK**. The settings will take effect.

Index